■ DRUGS
The Straight Facts

Codeine

DRUGS The Straight Facts

■ DRUGS
The Straight Facts

Codeine

Brigid M. Kane

Consulting Editor
David J. Triggle

University Professor
School of Pharmacy and Pharmaceutical Sciences
State University of New York at Buffalo

CHELSEA HOUSE
P U B L I S H E R S
An imprint of Infobase Publishing

Codeine

Chelsea House
An imprint of Infobase Publishing
132 West 31st Street
New York NY 10001

Library of Congress Cataloging-in-Publication Data

Kane, Brigid M.
   Codeine / Brigid M. Kane.
      p. cm.—(Drugs, the straight facts)
   Includes bibliographical references and index.
   ISBN 0-7910-8550-3 (hardcover)
   1. Codeine—Juvenile literature. I. Title. II. Series.
   RM666.C63K36 2006
   615'.7822—dc22   2006018947

Table of Contents

Acknowledgments

The author would like to thank John Zawadzki, Ph.D., for his invaluable insights and critical review of the manuscript, Desiree Little, Ph.D., for her editorial assistance, Xinxin Ding, Ph.D., for sharing his expertise in pharmacogenomics, Mike Zdeb and Justine McCarthy for their music connections, Stephen Immerwahr (founding member of the rock band Codeine), and to the high school students who agreed to read and comment on the individual chapter manuscripts—thank you Molly McAleese and Christopher Stanyon (Gloversville High School, Gloversville, New York), Francesca Sauchelli (St. Cassian School, Upper Montclair, New Jersey), and Andrew Kane (Manasquan High School, Manasquan, New Jersey). The author is also grateful to her family for their constant support.

The Use and Abuse of Drugs

The issues associated with drug use and abuse in contemporary society are vexing subjects, fraught with political agendas and ideals that often obscure essential information that teens need to know to have intelligent discussions about how to best deal with the problems associated with drug use and abuse. *Drugs: The Straight Facts* aims to provide this essential information through straightforward explanations of how an individual drug or group of drugs works in both therapeutic and non-therapeutic conditions; with historical information about the use and abuse of specific drugs with discussion of drug policies in the United States; and with an ample list of further reading.

From the start, the series uses the word "drug" to describe psychoactive substances that are used for medicinal or non-medicinal purposes. Included in this broad category are substances that are legal or illegal. It is worth noting that humans have used many of these substances for hundreds, if not thousands, of years. For example, traces of marijuana and cocaine have been found in Egyptian mummies; the use of peyote and Amanita fungi has long been a component of religious ceremonies worldwide; and alcohol production and consumption have been an integral part of many human cultures' social and religious ceremonies. One can speculate about why early human societies used such drugs, but very likely it was for the same reasons we do—namely, to relieve pain and to heal wounds. Perhaps, anything that could give people a break from the poor conditions and the fatigue associated with hard work was considered a welcome tonic. Life in premodern cultures was likely to be, in the memorable words of seventeenth-century English philosopher Thomas Hobbes, "poor, nasty, brutish, and short." One can also speculate about modern human societies' continued use and abuse of drugs. Whatever the reasons, the consequences of sustained drug use are not insignificant—addiction, unwanted side effects, overdose, and, for illegal, nonprescription drugs, incarceration, and drug wars—and must be dealt with by an informed citizenry.

The problem that faces our society today is how to break the connection between our demand for drugs and the willingness of largely outside countries to supply this highly profitable trade. This is the same problem we have faced since narcotics and cocaine were outlawed by the Harrison Narcotic Act of 1914, and we have yet to defeat it despite current expenditures in excess of approximately $20 billion per year on "the war on drugs" and the incarceration of a significant fraction of our citizens, particularly of minorities. The first step in meeting any challenge is to become informed about the nature of the challenge. The purpose of this series is to educate our readers so that they can make informed decisions about issues related to drugs and drug abuse.

SUGGESTED ADDITIONAL READING

Courtwright, David T. *Forces of Habit, Drugs and the Making of the Modern World*. Cambridge, Mass.: Harvard University Press, 2001. David T. Courtwright is professor of history at the University of North Florida.

Davenport-Hines, Richard. *The Pursuit of Oblivion: A Global History of Narcotics*. New York: Norton, 2002. The author is a professional historian and a member of the Royal Historical Society.

Huxley, Aldous. *Brave New World*. New York: Harper & Row, 1932. Huxley's book, written in 1932, paints a picture of a cloned society devoted only to the pursuit of happiness.

David J. Triggle, Ph.D.
University Professor
School of Pharmacy and Pharmaceutical Sciences
State University of New York at Buffalo

1

Medicinal and Cultural History

Codeine was first identified as a distinct compound in opium, the extract from the poppy plant, in 1832 by the French chemist Pierre-Jean Robiquet. Opium, also called raw or crude opium, is the dried milky juice obtained from the unripe capsules of the poppy plant, *Papaver somniferum*. The opium poppy is one of the oldest cultivated plants, dating back to around 3000 B.C., according to a cuneiform script referring to the opium poppy on Sumerian clay tablets. (Sumer, the oldest known civilization, was located in Mesopotamia, the land between the Tigris and Euphrates rivers in what is the southern part of modern day Iraq.) The Sumerians called the opium poppy "plant of joy," an allusion to opium's ability to relieve pain and induce a sense of well-being (**euphoria**). The label suggests that the Sumerians used opium for medicinal purposes (pain relief, or **analgesia**) and recreation (for its euphoric, or "feel-good" qualities). Hippocrates (ca. 460–377 B.C.), the Greek physician and "the father of medicine," used opium as a therapeutic; he wrote of its usefulness for inducing numbness or **stupor** in patients with excruciating pain around 400 B.C. Much has been written on the history of opium, and a fascinating timeline can be found at http://www.pbs.org/wgbh/pages/frontline/shows/heroin/etc/history.html.

Codeine is one of 40 individual chemical compounds (specifically, **alkaloid** compounds) found in opium. Only a few of the opiate alkaloids are used medically: the analgesics (painkillers) morphine

Figure 1.1 Afghan farmers collect opium in Kandahar, Afghanistan. © AP/Wide World Photos

and codeine, and the antipsychotic drug papaverine. Morphine is the most abundant alkaloid contained in opium (8-17 percent), followed by codeine (0.7-5 percent). (Morphine, named after Morpheus, the Greek god of dreams, was first isolated from opium only a few years earlier than codeine, in 1806 by the German pharmacist, Friedrich Wilhelm Adam Serturner.) Although crude opium had been used throughout the world for centuries, by the mid-19th century preparations of pure alkaloids were being used medicinally. Today, because of codeine's low concentration in opium, the drug is manufactured from morphine for commercial use.

Figure 1.2 Opium poppies. Courtesy Drug Enforcement Administration

CODEINE'S CURRENT POPULARITY

The medicinal, or therapeutic, uses of codeine are to relieve pain, to suppress cough, and to control diarrhea (see Chapters 2 and 3). Because of its usefulness and availability as an oral medication (as opposed to an injectable medication), codeine may be the single most commonly dispensed prescription medicine in the United States. In 2004, the last full year for which data are available, more than 157 million prescriptions were written for codeine. This number of prescriptions was the highest of the 20 most-prescribed therapeutic categories. Prescriptions for codeine, and codeine-containing medicines, accounted for $3.3 billion dollars of pharmaceutical sales in the United States in 2004. Preliminary data show that the number of prescriptions for codeine for the nine-month period January to September 2005 is more than 164 million, so the drug continues to gain in popularity.

As you may be aware, in addition to codeine's legitimate medicinal uses described above, codeine is often abused as a recreational drug (see Chapters 5 and 6). The "high," or state of euphoria associated with codeine is the reason for the drug's popularity on the street. Some have described the high associated with codeine as a woozy and syrupy feeling. According to the Drug Enforcement Agency (DEA), a part of the U.S. Department of Justice, codeine is now ranked among the top three most frequently identified, illegally trafficked analgesics (painkillers) in the country. Chapter 6 discusses codeine as a controlled substance, a designation referring to the drug's potential for abuse and addiction and thus the need for regulated ("controlled") dispensing and use.

TERMINOLOGY

- Opium is the dried milky juice obtained from the unripe capsules of the poppy plant, *Papaver somniferum*. The word *opium* comes from the Greek word for sap, or juice, a reference to the substance from the seed capsules of *Papaver somniferum* from which the drug is derived.

- Opiate refers to any drug derived from opium. Opiates include codeine, morphine, and papaverine.

- Opioid refers to any compound that acts like morphine, the most abundant alkaloid compound in opium. The term *opioid* includes substances that are derived from plants (such as morphine and codeine), those that occur naturally in the body (such as endorphins and enkephalins), and synthesized compounds (such as heroin and fentanyl). [Endorphins and enkephalins are discussed in Chapters 2 and 3. Fentanyl is discussed in Chapter 3.]

Opiates prevalent in drug misuse deaths

Almost two-thirds of all drug deaths in Philadelphia and neighboring metro areas were accidental. A large number of deaths stemmed from opiates like heroin.

Drug-related deaths for Philadelphia metropolitan area

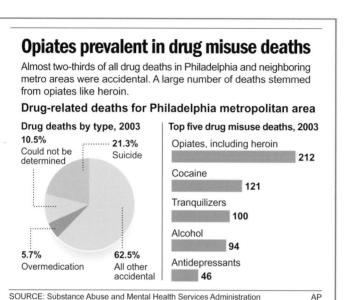

Drug deaths by type, 2003

10.5%
Could not be determined

21.3%
Suicide

5.7%
Overmedication

62.5%
All other accidental

Top five drug misuse deaths, 2003

Opiates, including heroin
212

Cocaine
121

Tranquilizers
100

Alcohol
94

Antidepressants
46

SOURCE: Substance Abuse and Mental Health Services Administration   AP

Figure 1.3 © AP

2

Current Medical Use

WHO TAKES CODEINE? WHEN AND WHY?

As we mentioned in the previous chapter, the three most common prescribed uses for codeine are as an analgesic (painkiller), a cough suppressant, and to control diarrhea. This chapter will explain these drug actions, or effects, on the body in further detail, and some of the potential consequences of using codeine more frequently or at higher doses than recommended for medicinal purposes. Codeine's popularity as a recreational drug is rooted in its narcotic qualities. Medically speaking, a narcotic is any drug or substance that produces a generalized depression of brain functioning, which manifests as insensibility or stupor. The term narcotic was originally a medical term and was restricted to opioids.

COUGH SUPPRESSION

Codeine suppresses the cough reflex by depressing the cough center in the brain, located in the medulla oblongata, the lowermost portion of the brain stem that controls involuntary processes such as heartbeat, respiration—and coughing. Codeine is used for "unproductive" or "non-productive" cough, which refers to a cough that does not produce mucus or phlegm from the respiratory airways or from the trachea and bronchi of the lungs. With an unproductive cough, nothing is cleared from the respiratory airways. Unproductive cough can be disturbing enough that it prevents or interferes with sleep, leaving a person fatigued or exhausted. On the other hand, if a

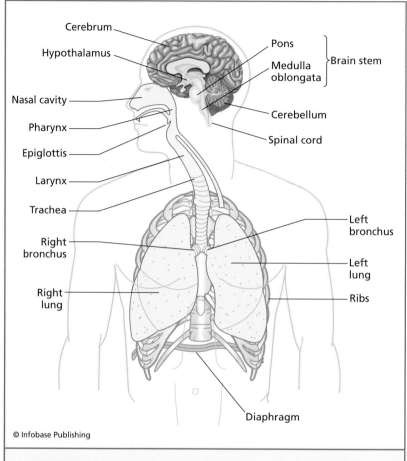

Figure 2.1 Diagram of the brain inside the human body. The medulla oblongata controls the cough reflex and serves as the "cough center" of the body.

person has a persistent productive cough (a "cough with results," so to speak), it generally signals an infection or underlying condition that needs the attention of a health care professional. A cough suppressant is not generally used for patients with productive cough because you don't want to interfere with the body's attempt to rid itself of mucus. Depending on the medical condition and the exact

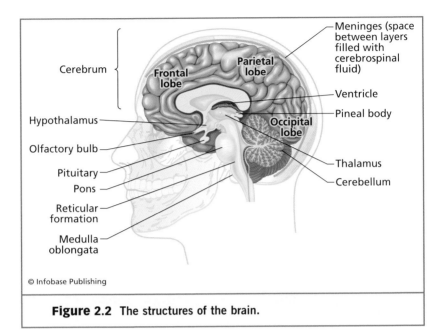

© Infobase Publishing

Figure 2.2 The structures of the brain.

circumstances surrounding a patient with productive cough—such as the length of time that the patient has had the cough—the doctor may want to collect a sample of mucus expelled by the patient for microscopic examination.

A SPOONFUL OF MEDICINE FOR COUGH

Codeine is often able to suppress cough at lower doses than those used to relieve pain. Codeine is most effective when given orally, rather than by injection. A 10- or 20-milligram oral dose of codeine is not particularly effective for killing pain in adults, but it is generally good for dramatically reducing cough. For cough suppression, codeine is a common ingredient in a cough syrup or other liquid **formulation**. Codeine for cough suppression is also supplied in tablet form, again usually in combination with other ingredients. Codeine-containing tablets require a prescription from a clinician. Generally speaking, most states allow the sale of cough syrups containing less than 10 milligrams (mg) of codeine without a prescription.

continued on page 20

THE COUGH REFLEX

Coughing is a reflex action, or involuntary movement, in which the body tries to expel foreign material (such as dust, a bug, or excess mucus secretions) from the respiratory airways (specifically the trachea, or windpipe, and the bronchi, also called bronchial tubes, of the lungs.)

The cough reflex involves the muscle surrounding the bronchi and both branches of our nervous system—the central nervous system, or CNS, which includes the brain and spinal cord, and the peripheral nervous system, which includes the network of nerves that convey voluntary and involuntary sensory and motor signals from all parts of the body to and from the brain and spinal cord. Precisely how the cough reflex works is not completely understood. The initial stimulus of the cough reflex may be some kind of irritation of the mucus lining of the bronchi; the irritation may be a trigger for the bronchi to narrow, and this action (constriction) then stimulates cough receptors that are studded along the trachea and bronchi. Peripheral nerve fibers (of the peripheral nervous system) transmit the signal from the cough receptors to the cough center in the CNS. Several types of drugs are able to interfere with the complex reflex action, including codeine (which acts on the CNS) and bronchodilators (which act on the muscle surrounding the bronchi to reverse the constricting action). Bronchodilators are commonly used for asthma and allergies.

Codeine is especially useful for relieving painful cough because, in addition to its action as a cough suppressant, codeine is an analgesic. (We'll take a closer look at its pain relief action below.) Codeine also has a sedative, or calming, effect, which may be desirable for patients who are not getting enough rest because their unproductive cough is keeping them awake. Codeine also dries out the mucous lining of the respiratory airways, which may be beneficial to a patient with excessive runny mucus discharge, or it could be not so good if the patient

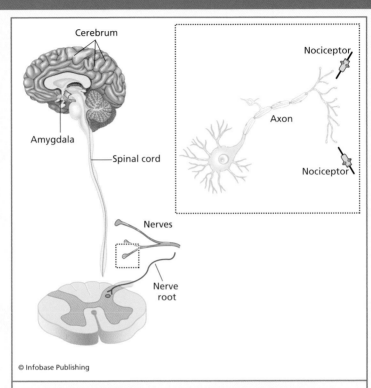

© Infobase Publishing

Figure 2.3 Nerves are complex structures that carry electrical information throughout our bodies. Virtually every tissue is connected to the central nervous system through nerves. This diagram shows the path of a message of pain to the brain.

has heavy, thick mucus; such secretions need to be expelled and because codeine suppresses the cough reflex, it prevents expulsion of the thick mucus, which likely contains cellular debris and debris from partially digested microorganisms. (It is not essential or critical that thick mucus be expelled in all settings; heavy, thick mucus can be problematic for patients with airway obstructions or breathing problems or bedridden patients with serious or persistent infections.

Depending on the amount or strength of codeine in the product, the cough syrup may require a prescription. In most states, tablets that contain 10 mg of codeine are considered "prescription-strength," meaning that they require a prescription to be purchased. State laws vary as to whether they require a doctor's prescription for codeine-containing products. One state may allow a product to be purchased over the counter (as opposed to behind the pharmacist's or druggist's counter), while a neighboring state may require that a pharmacist dispense the medicine by prescription only.

As with all drugs, codeine has some undesirable effects in addition to its therapeutic effects. At the usual cough suppressing doses (see below), codeine may cause **nausea**—the medical term for upset stomach accompanied by the sensation of queasiness—which makes you feel as if you are about to regurgitate (vomit, or "throw up"). Codeine may cause vomiting

ANTITUSSIVES

The word *tussive* comes from the Latin *tussis*, meaning cough. An antitussive agent, then, is a drug that suppresses or prevents cough. Codeine and dextromethorphan are the most commonly used antitussives. Other opioids are also effective antitussive agents, but are not used as medicines to suppress cough.

Codeine
Hydrocodone
Dextromethorphan
Hydromorphone
Chlophedianol
Methadone
Levopropoxyphene
Morphine
Noscapine

Source: Beers, M.H., and R. Berkow (eds). *The Merck Manual of Diagnosis and Therapy*. 17th edition. Whitehouse Station, NJ: Merck Research Laboratories, 1999.

and **constipation** (hardening of the **stools**, causing infrequent or difficult bowel movements, or **defecation**). Chapter 4 discusses codeine's side effects, or **toxicities**, in more detail. Chapter 3 discusses exactly how codeine exerts its various biological actions once the drug is swallowed.

CODEINE TABLETS AND CAPSULES

The usual codeine dose and timing of dose separation for children is 1 to 1.5 milligrams (mg) of codeine per body weight (in kilograms) per day, but given as several doses every 4 to 6 hours. The accepted medical or pharmacological shorthand is 1-1.5 mg/kg/day, q4-6h, where "q" stands for every, and "h" represents hours. The usual "adult" (older than 13 years of age) dose and schedule is 10-20 mg, q4-6h, as needed, although 60-mg doses may occasionally be needed.

Brontex® and Guiatussin® with Codeine are two brand-name cough suppressants available in tablet form. They contain 10 mg of codeine plus the expectorant guaifenesin. (An **expectorant** helps expel mucus secretions from the airways.)

CODEINE IN LIQUID FORMULATION

Cough syrups that contain codeine may also contain one of several drugs categorized as expectorants. To help the medicine go down, most cough syrups are "palatable" and "aromatic" (at least that's what the advertisements say). The following brand names contain 10 mg of codeine: Cheracol® with Codeine Syrup; Tussi-Organidin®-NR and Tussi-Organidin®-S NR; Robitussin A-C® Syrup; Guiatussin AC® Syrup; Gani-Tuss® NR.

ANALGESIA (PAIN RELIEF)

The word *analgesia* is from the Greek: *an-*, meaning not or without, + *algesis*, sense of pain. Codeine is more potent than other pain-relieving medications, such as aspirin and ibuprofen, but less potent than the really serious painkillers—morphine, oxycodone + acetaminophen, hydromorphone. When a therapeutic dose of codeine is given to people in pain, they report that the pain is less intense, or vanishes completely (for a time). Depending on the medical situation, codeine can be an effective pain reliever for injury to muscles and/or bone, the acute pain ("flare") of arthritis, some post-operative pain (including tooth extraction or other dental surgery), migraine and tension headaches, pain associated with cancer, and post-episiotomy pain (episiotomy is a surgical procedure sometimes necessary during childbirth).

Codeine relieves pain by acting on specific receptors studded along the so-called pain pathways in the central nervous system (CNS). Figure 2.4 illustrates how pain signals travel to the brain from the spinal cord. The spinal cord receives sensory input from peripheral nerves that extend from the actual site of pain. Codeine dampens the pain signals from the spinal cord that are transmitted to an area of the brain called the **amygdala** and passed to various areas of the **cerebrum** where they are "translated." (The cerebrum of the brain is where higher thought processing takes place.)

Codeine also activates pain-control circuits that descend from the section of the brain called the midbrain to the spinal cord, causing the release of naturally produced opioids called endorphins and enkephalins. The endorphins and enkaphalins bind to and activate receptors on cells in the spinal cord that prevent the transmission of pain signals. As discussed in Chapter 3, endorphins and enkephalins are your body's natural chemicals that allow you to "feel no pain."

Pain is actually difficult to define. In medicine, it is characterized by its intensity: mild, moderate, or severe. Codeine is commonly used to relieve pain that is of mild-to-moderate intensity. Codeine is also used to treat acute pain, or pain that is associated with tissue injury that lasts less than one month. An example of acute pain is the intense pain experienced after having a tooth removed. In addition, codeine is used to treat chronic pain, such as the constant, unrelenting pain that accompanies some types of advanced cancer. Chronic pain can also be caused by an injury, but it doesn't wane; rather, it continues after healing is complete. Although chronic pain is typically associated with cancer, it is also seen with such disorders as arthritis, **sickle cell anemia**, lower back pain, and headache.

Codeine is available in tablet form, alone or in combination with other analgesics, such as aspirin and acetaminophen. When combined with another analgesic, the pain-relieving effect of the two analgesics is additive. The use of a couple of analgesics in combination has an advantage over using codeine as a single-agent: A lower dose of codeine can be used in combination products, and therefore side effects, which tend to increase at higher doses, are avoided or minimized. The therapeutic strategy for treating pain is depicted in an "analgesic ladder," a three-step guideline for choosing the right pain medication, developed by the World Health Organization. (See Figure 2.4).

CODEINE FORMULATIONS

As mentioned, codeine is most effective when it is given by mouth. When used as an analgesic, codeine is often given as a tablet. The recommended oral dose of codeine in adults is 60 mg q3-4 h. In children, the oral dose is 1 mg per kilogram of body weight q3-4h. Codeine has a relatively short duration of action (3 to 4 hours), and it is this duration that determines the recommended dosing frequency. Codeine is available as a single-agent tablet (for oral administration in a variety of doses). Codeine, however, is also manufactured as a controlled-release tablet, a special formulation that slowly releases codeine from the inactive ingredients in the pill. The controlled-release formulation has a longer duration of action. Also, as previously mentioned, codeine is combined, or co-formulated, with other analgesic agents, such as acetaminophen (Tylenol® with codeine), for added pain relief.

ANTIDIARRHEAL

Codeine is one of the most potent and effective drugs for the **symptomatic** treatment of diarrhea, a condition marked by

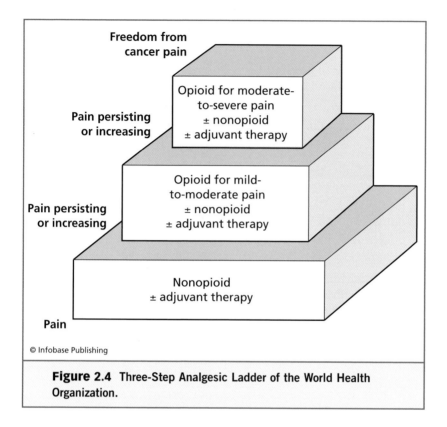

Figure 2.4 Three-Step Analgesic Ladder of the World Health Organization.

unusual frequency of bowel movements (usually more fluid than solid). Diarrhea is caused by a variety of factors. A few of the more common causes of loose, watery stools and abdominal cramps are mild food poisoning, **gastrointestinal** infections from viruses or bacteria, some medications, some foods, and some food additives, such as artificial sweeteners.

The antidiarrheal activity of codeine results from two actions. First, there is a decrease in the propulsive contractile activity of the small and large intestines, which delays the forward movement of the contents of the intestines. Second, codeine causes an increase in the absorption of water from the intestinal contents. These gastrointestinal effects are mediated by specific opioid receptors in the gut (as we will see in

Chapter 3), but there may be a central nervous system component like the cough center in the brain that contributes to these effects as well.

For the treatment of diarrhea, 15 to 30 mg of codeine is typically given two to three times per day until bowel movements return to normal. Because of the risk of addiction, however, codeine as an antidiarrheal drug is dispensed sparingly. Constipation (the opposite of diarrhea—there is no movement) is considered an unwanted side effect of codeine when it is used for its analgesic effect. (This is discussed in Chapter 4.)

3

Medicinal Chemistry and Pharmacology

To fully understand how codeine exerts its various actions in the body after being ingested, it is necessary to know the chemical make-up of codeine. Before we examine the codeine molecule, though, let's take a brief look at the systematic way in which drugs are studied and tested. Very broadly, medicinal chemists define and characterize the physical and chemical properties of substances that have a potential for use as drugs or are already being used as drugs.

Closely related to **medicinal chemistry** is the field of **pharmacology**, which is the study of how and why drugs work (or don't work) in the body. Pharmacologic studies critically examine the intended and unintended actions of drugs *in vitro* (literally, "in glass," the test tube) and *in vivo* (in a living organism). Prior to the study of drug action in the human body, pharmacologists and toxicologists will conduct *in vitro* and animal experiments to characterize a drug's action in these systems and to weed out any obviously inappropriate drug candidates for use in humans. (This brief background is meant to give you a sense of how medicinal chemistry and pharmacology intersect in the research world.)

For codeine to work in the body, the drug needs to gain access to the bloodstream after being ingested or injected so that it can be delivered to its anatomic target site of action. After being absorbed into the circulation, the blood transports, or distributes, codeine to various parts of the body. But **absorption** can be a tricky thing. Absorption of codeine (or any drug) into the bloodstream is dependent upon numerous drug characteristics, such as: (1) aqueous **solubility** (Does the drug dissolve in water? Is it poorly soluble, or insoluble in water?); (2) lipid solubility (To what degree is the drug able to dissolve in fat-containing fluids?); (3) the relative ease of or resistance to degradation by **enzymes** (such as might occur in the mouth or stomach); (4) the drug's formulation (Can it be manufactured as a pill or must it be injected?); and (5) the drug's degree of **ionization** (What electrical charge is associated with the drug *in vivo*?). Codeine's lipid solubility and degree of ionization are critical factors that determine whether the drug can be readily transported across cell membranes. (Cell membranes function to keep things in and out of a cell's interior, and are made up of double layers of fat, or lipid, molecules surrounding a watery interior.)

Together, the chemistry of codeine and the drug's absorption into the bloodstream, distribution to various compartments and tissues in the body, **metabolism** (breakdown of the "**parent compound**" into smaller molecules, or **metabolites**), and **excretion** are intimately related to how codeine exerts its medicinal or therapeutic effects. Codeine's chemical properties and pharmacologic characteristics explain how, figuratively speaking, a "spoonful" of codeine can relieve pain, suppress cough, or act as an antidiarrheal. The medicinal chemistry and pharmacology of codeine can also shed light on why specific side effects (the unintended, undesirable, and unwanted effects) associated with codeine occur. Codeine's side effects, or toxicities, are discussed in the next chapter.

MEDICINAL CHEMISTRY

The chemical name of codeine—methylmorphine—is rather revealing, especially for those who know **organic chemistry** (the study of carbon and compounds containing carbon, which are referred to as organic compounds). As with morphine, the structure of codeine contains a five-ring carbon nucleus (phenanthrene). The prefix in *methylmorphine* tells us how codeine is chemically related to morphine: There is a methyl group (three hydrogen atoms bonded to a single carbon atom, designated CH_3) attached to the morphine molecule (Figure 3.1). Amazingly, this small group of atoms — CH_3 — is responsible for the physical, chemical, and pharmacologic properties that distinguish codeine from morphine.

Like morphine, codeine is extracted from natural opium, obtained from the poppy plant (*Papaver somniferum*). Only when it was first discovered and tested was codeine purified directly from opium (see Chapter 1). Today **pharmaceutical-grade** codeine is synthesized from morphine through the relatively simple chemical modification process of **methylation**, whereby CH_3 replaces a hydrogen atom on the morphine molecule. The chemical substitution reaction that takes place (H for CH_3) does so at a specific location on the morphine molecule (Figure 3.1); if the substitution were to occur elsewhere on

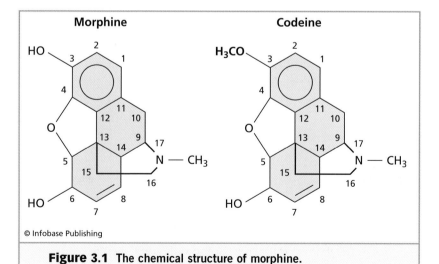

© Infobase Publishing

Figure 3.1 The chemical structure of morphine.

the molecule, the resulting compound would be something other than codeine.

The seemingly small difference in chemical composition between codeine and morphine makes a significant difference in terms of chemical behavior and, ultimately, the drug's action in the body. Apparently, the three-dimensional structure of codeine differs just enough from morphine to lower its **affinity** for binding to molecules in the body that control the sensation of pain. (These opioid receptors will be discussed below.) In other words, codeine is a less potent painkiller compared with morphine, due in part to codeine's 3D structure. Table 3.1 indicates that the inclusion of a methyl group on the morphine molecule affects several physical properties. Who (besides a medicinal chemist or biochemist) would imagine that the addition of a single methyl group would alter a compound's solubility and thereby affect its ability to readily cross cell membranes and access different body compartments?

Although codeine is manufactured in formulations in which it is the sole active ingredient (codeine phosphate oral

(continued on page 32)

Table 3.1 Physical Properties of Codeine and Morphine

Formula	Molecular weight	Melting point (°C)	Boiling point (°C)	Solubility
Codeine $C_{18}H_{21}NO_3$	299.37	157-158.5	250	alcohol: vs ether: s water: s
Morphine $C_{17}H_{19}NO_3$	285.35	254-256.4	—	alcohol: sl ether: i water: i
s = soluble; vs = very soluble; sl = slightly soluble; i = insoluble				
Source: CRC Handbook of Chemistry and Physics, 87th edition, 2006.				

ORAL DRUG DELIVERY

Codeine is most often given orally, as a tablet, capsule, syrup, or liquid solution. However, there are other oral routes of delivery. For example, the potent opioid analgesic, fentanyl (a chemically synthesized opioid), can be delivered in a lollipop or lozenge formulation. An interesting case study reported by King, et al. of a patient who experienced a seizure highlights an unusual oral route of delivery:

"A 26-year-old baker had witnessed a first tonic-clonic seizure. He was delirious and terrified afterwards, struggling against hallucinatory figures. He was taken by ambulance to hospital, but when he arrived, his delirium had resolved. Clinical examination,

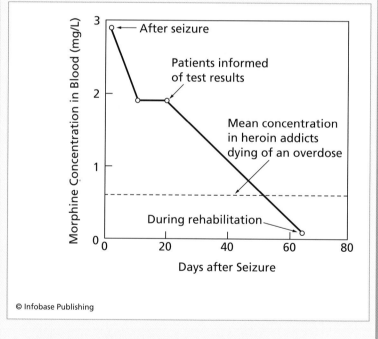

© Infobase Publishing

Figure 3.2 This line graph demonstrates the amounts of morphine and codeine in the blood, measured by high performance liquid chromatography.

electroencephalograph, and brain magnetic resonance imaging were normal."

Neurologic examination and tests, including brain magnetic resonance imaging (MRI) suggested some kind of drug toxicity, but the patient at first denied having taken any drugs.

"However, the following week his business partner informed us that increased quantities of poppy seed had been ordered for the bakery, up to 25 kg every week, whereas only 3 kg were required. Poppy seeds contain morphine and codeine. Blood stored in the laboratory on the day of the seizure was found to contain a very high concentration of morphine. High concentrations were

Figure 3.3 Opium poppy seed capsule. © Dr. Jeremy Burgess/Photo Researchers, Inc.

subsequently found in blood and urine over a three-week period... When informed of these results, he admitted to drinking poppy tea at night in the bakery. He first learned of this practice from other bakers during his apprenticeship ... Bakers may be at occupational risk of poppy-seed addiction."

This vignette is instructive on several counts. Getting the right dose delivered is critical for therapeutic effectiveness and to avoid harmful side effects or toxicities. Researchers who work on drug delivery in the field of pharmaceutical science know this well. A concoction such as poppy tea delivers an unreliable and uncontrolled amount (concentration) of morphine and codeine. Pharmaceutical-grade medicines—whether pills, lollipops, or patches—are designed to deliver a precise amount of drug that has been calculated and repeatedly tested and verified.

(continued from page 29)

solution or codeine sulfate tablets), it is most widely used in combination with other analgesic drugs such as aspirin and acetaminophen (e.g., Tylenol®) and/or in combination with agents that thin out mucous secretions to control chest congestion due to colds and allergies, i.e. expectorants.

CODEINE FORMULATIONS

Codeine, either alone or in combination with other drugs, is given orally as a tablet or capsule or in liquid form (including as syrup). Codeine can also be "delivered" via intramuscular injection, usually for patients unable to swallow because of a medical condition such as throat cancer. One of the interesting pharmacologic characteristics of codeine is the drug's **potency**

Table 3.2 **Select Medications That Contain Codeine**

Brand	Ingredients other than codeine*	Formulation	Use
Tylenol® with codeine	acetaminophen	Tablets, liquid	Relief of acute pain of mild-to-moderate intensity
Fiorinal® with codeine	butalbital, aspirin, caffeine	Capsules	Relief of tension headache caused by stress, muscle contraction in the head, neck, shoulder area
Phenergan® with codeine	promethazine	Liquid	Relief of persistent cough, other symptoms of allergies and common cold
Tussi-Organidin®-NR	guaifenesin	Liquid	Relief of cough, chest congestion
Brontex®	guaifenesin	Tablets	Relief of cough, chest congestion

*Acetaminophen is a non-narcotic **antipyretic** (fever-reducing) analgesic that is used to reduce pain and fever. Butalbital is a sedative **barbiturate**. Aspirin is a non-narcotic antipyretic analgesic used to reduce pain and fever. Caffeine is a stimulant. Guaifenesin is an expectorant, used to thin and loosen mucus in the respiratory airways, making it easier to cough up and expel the mucus. Promethazine is an **antihistamine** that helps to reduce itching and swelling and dries up secretions from the nose, eyes, and throat. It also has sedative effects and helps control nausea and vomiting.

Source: MedlinePlus: http://www.medlineplus.com; RxList: http://www.rxlist.com; Drug Digest: http://www.drugdigest.org; HealthDigest: http://healthdigest.org.

as an oral medication compared with its **parenteral** (injected) formulation. Codeine is roughly 60 percent more potent when it is given orally as a tablet or liquid versus as an injection into muscle (intramuscular). Thus, codeine is a stronger painkiller when it is taken orally, and its administration is therefore almost always by the oral route. This is not the case for the large majority of drugs. Most drugs that are given by injection are almost always more potent than their orally administered counterparts, primarily because parenteral formulations bypass the enzymes in the gastrointestinal tract (oral cavity, stomach, and intestines); these enzymes can degrade pills and ultimately reduce their effectiveness. Furthermore, parenteral formulations avoid the acidic environment (low pH) of the stomach, which again can result in degradation of some pill formulations.

ONCE THE MEDICINE GOES DOWN

We have established that codeine is most commonly taken as an oral medication. So, once a pill or liquid suspension containing codeine is swallowed, what happens? Figure 3.4 gives a simplified answer.

After ingestion of a therapeutic dose, codeine is readily absorbed from the gastrointestinal tract with the maximum analgesic effect occurring after approximately one hour. Although specific foods, beverages, herbs or natural products, and other simultaneously administered medicines can affect the absorption of various drugs, very few have been noted to affect codeine absorption. Some evidence reveals that herbs with large amounts of **tannins** may interfere with the absorption of codeine and should not be taken together with codeine or codeine-containing products. (Tannins, including tannic acid, are compounds found in the fruit and bark of certain plants, such as tea, that give plants an astringent or puckery taste; they are used in dyeing, tanning leather, and as an astringent to bind tissue in medicine.)

Like the food and beverages we eat and drink, the drugs we take are metabolized, or broken down, in our bodies by

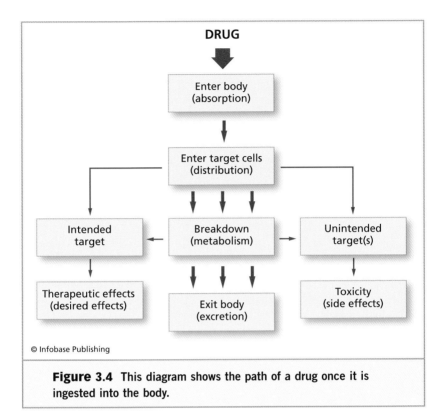

DRUG

Enter body
(absorption)

Enter target cells
(distribution)

Intended
target

Breakdown
(metabolism)

Unintended
target(s)

Therapeutic effects
(desired effects)

Exit body
(excretion)

Toxicity
(side effects)

© Infobase Publishing

Figure 3.4 This diagram shows the path of a drug once it is ingested into the body.

enzymes. In fact, the same enzymatic pathways and transport systems that are used for the metabolism of food are also used to break down drugs and environmental toxins and plant products or herbal supplements. These enzymes, the **cytochrome P450** "superfamily" of enzymes, are found in almost all tissues of the body, but the highest levels are located in the liver.

After codeine is absorbed into the bloodstream, it is transported to the liver, the body's detoxifying organ and the primary organ responsible for the metabolism of many drugs, including all the opioid analgesics. Codeine is rapidly and extensively metabolized in the liver. The extensive metabolism of codeine by the liver means that this drug needs to be carefully monitored when given to patients with liver disease, such as patients with **hepatitis C virus** infection or liver cancer. A damaged or diseased liver does not function as well as a healthy liver, and therefore, depending on the extent of tissue damage, drugs normally metabolized by the liver will be metabolized incompletely or slower than in an individual with a healthy liver. Slowing down the metabolism of codeine means that the drug could accumulate and/or it is not cleared from the body within the "normal" timeframe; this can have the same effect as an overdose.

Metabolic studies of codeine indicate that approximately 10 percent of codeine (whose chemical name is methylmorphine) is converted to its active metabolite, morphine; it is this small fraction of morphine that provides codeine's analgesic effect.

The metabolic conversion of codeine occurs by **demethylation**, a process aptly described by the name: the methyl group (CH_3) on the codeine molecule (shown in Figure 3.1) is simply

HERBS THAT MAY BE AFFECTED BY CODEINE ABSORPTION*

Green tea *(Camellia sinensis)*

Black tea

Uva ursi *(Arctostaphylos uva-ursi)*

Black walnut *(Juglans nigra)*

Oak *(Quercus spp.)*

Red raspberry *(Rubus idaeus)*

Witch hazel *(Hamamelis virginiana)*

* These herbs contain high levels of tannins (plant products that have an astringent taste). Source: Yale New Haven Health. Available online. URL: http://yalenewhavenhealth.org/library/healthguide/en-us/Cam/topic.asp?hwid=hn-1197005. Accessed May 20, 2006.

lopped off. Metabolic studies conducted *in vitro* and in laboratory animals have identified the specific **hepatic** (liver) enzyme responsible for the breakdown of codeine: CYP2D6, which is one of the approximately 15 cytochrome P450 enzymes. Some people have **dysfunctional** or inactive CYP2D6 enzymes, which results in the incomplete or inadequate metabolism of food and drugs that are normally metabolized by these enzymes. In the case of codeine, if the CYP2D6 enzymes are dysfunctional, the drug will be poorly metabolized (the demethylation to morphine is thwarted); not surprisingly, people with dysfunctional CYP2D6 enzymes have a poor response to codeine's therapeutic effects. In other words, the drug doesn't work for them.

It turns out that there is quite a bit of **variability** in the **genes** that encode the cytochrome P450 enzymes that are responsible for the metabolism of many commonly used medications. In fact, the genetic variability explains why a particular drug at a particular dose works wonders in some people and doesn't work in others and, equally important, why some people have bad or adverse reactions to a particular drug at a particular dose while others don't. The discovery of the variability in these genes between people has led to the creation of new specialties in pharmacology: **pharmacogenetics** and **pharmacogenomics**. Pharmaco*genetics* (*pharmaco*, relating to drugs or medicine + *genetics*, referring to the study of inherited traits encoded by genes) is devoted to establishing the link between the variation in human genes and the variation in the response to a given drug between people. Pharmaco*genomics* (*pharmaco*, relating to drugs or medicine + *genomics*, the study of the genome, or complete genetic make-up, of an organism) is the analysis of an individual's genes to predict their response to a given drug. Pharmacogenomics is considered by some to be a stepping stone to personalized medicine. Chapter 4 discusses the relationship between the variation in genes and the variation in a drug's side effects between people, another emerging specialty

THE LANGUAGE OF GENOMICS

The recent explosion of information from the study of the human genome has impacted pharmacology in a big way. Genes are made up long strings of DNA molecules (see below) that are highly coiled and compacted into structures called chromosomes. Humans have 23 pairs of chromosomes.

What's a genome? The complete genetic material, or collection of genes, of an organism. Thanks to the Human Genome Project, we now know that the human genome consists of approximately 20,000 to 30,000 genes. (Prior to completion of the Human Genome Project in April 2003, it was believed that the human genome contained approximately 100,000 genes.)

What's a gene? The most fundamental unit of heredity; genes carry the instructions for making all the molecules in an organism and the traits that are passed from parent to offspring. Genes are made up long strings of DNA molecules that are highly coiled and compacted into structures called chromosomes found in the nucleus of all cells.

What's DNA? Deoxyribonucleic acid, the helical ladderlike chain of molecules that makes up genes. DNA consists of a sugar molecule called deoxyribose (it is somewhat related to glucose), a nitrogen-containing molecule called a base, and phosphate atoms bonded to the other two components. It is the sequence of base pairs (one base on each strand) in DNA that determines the end-product (e.g., protein). The human genome—the entire DNA content of a human being—contains approximately 3 billion base pairs.

in pharmacology called **toxicogenomics** (*toxico*, relating to poisons or toxic substances + *genomics*, the study of the genome of an organism).

Food, other drugs, and even herbal remedies or natural products that are taken at or about the same time can affect the metabolism of codeine. If codeine's metabolism is affected, its therapeutic effects and side effects may be affected as well. Food appears to have only a minor effect on codeine metabolism. (Although grapefruit juice affects the metabolism of numerous drugs, it does not affect codeine metabolism. See Figure 3.5.) Some drugs, however, that are metabolized by the same cytochrome P450 enzyme as codeine (CYP2D6) or interfere with CYP2D6 activity can thwart codeine's metabolism to such a degree that it makes the usual therapeutic dose of codeine less effective than it would be if codeine were taken alone. The drug fluoxetine, or Prozac®, an antidepressant, for example, significantly slows down or inhibits CYP2D6's metabolizing activity, and therefore, when a patient is taking Prozac® and codeine, the analgesic effect of codeine is reduced.

Although the fields of pharmacogenetics and pharmacogenomics are relatively new, a picture of the degree of variability in the genes responsible for drug metabolism is beginning to emerge. Among Caucasians, approximately 5 percent to 10 percent of the population have dysfunctional or inactive CYP2D6 enzymes (called CYP2D6 poor metabolizers); among Asians, approximately 1 percent are CYP2D6 poor metabolizers; and among Blacks, 0 to 20 percent are CYP2D6 poor metabolizers. This means that the CYP2D6 poor metabolizers in each of these racial groups will reap little if any of codeine's analgesic effect. Health care professionals need to know this so that they can instruct patients to let them know if the codeine works after taking it for a few days. If the patient reports that his or her pain doesn't abate, then the clinician can prescribe a different painkiller. It is hoped that ongoing and future research will provide data on additional ethnic groups.

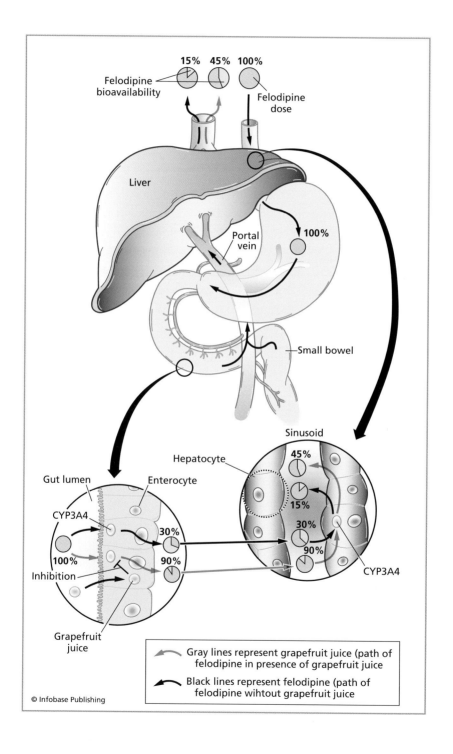

Felodipine bioavailability — 15% 45% 100%

Felodipine dose

Liver

Portal vein

100%

Small bowel

Sinusoid

Hepatocyte — 45% 15%

Gut lumen

Enterocyte

CYP3A4

30%

100%

90%

30%

90%

Inhibition

CYP3A4

Grapefruit juice

Gray lines represent grapefruit juice (path of felodipine in presence of grapefruit juice

Black lines represent felodipine (path of felodipine wihtout grapefruit juice

Because codeine is excreted chiefly by the kidneys (as determined by chemical analysis of the urine following administration of the drug), patients with diminished **renal** (kidney) function or renal disease may have problems with the **clearance** of codeine from their body. If not properly cleared, codeine and one or more of its metabolites, such as morphine, may accumulate in the body. An accumulation of morphine could result in the development of symptoms of opioid overdose (e.g., stupor, **coma**, and **cyanosis**, a bluish skin color due to an excessive lack of deoxygenated **hemoglobin** in the blood). Drug clearance and elimination are usually measured in hours. The **half-life** of a drug (the amount of time it takes for half of the starting dose of a drug to be eliminated from the body) is determined during the early research phases of a new drug to ensure that it does not accumulate in the body's tissues. A portion of the drug will be metabolized, but the remainder is eliminated from the body. (You could say that a twist on Newton's Law of Gravity applies: Just as what goes up must come down, so what goes in, must come out.) The average half-life of codeine in the blood **plasma** is two to four hours. A drug's half-life also tells us how long the drug can be expected to be effective and when another dose should be given. As we learned in Chapter 2, a typical adult dose for codeine as an analgesic is 30 to 60 mg *every three to four hours.* Whether another dose is needed every three hours or every four hours depends on the individual patient, which in turn,

(opposite page) **Figure 3.5** In this diagram, felodipine, an opioid, is ingested along with grapefruit juice. The CYP3A enzymes in the intestinal epithelium extensively metabolize felodipine during its absorption and on average, only 30 percent of the drug enters the portal vein. In the liver, the drug is further metabolized so that only 15 percent of the dose is bioavailable. The grapefruit juice selectively inhibits the CYP3A in the enterocyte, with the net result being an increase in the oral bioavailability of felodipine by a factor of three.

depends on such factors as the proper functioning of CYP2D6 enzymes or body weight.

DRUG ACTION

Codeine and other opioids, as well as naturally occurring substances in the body known as opioid **peptides**, the endorphins and enkephalins, bind with the opioid receptors in a lock-and-key fashion to produce a multitude of effects, such as analgesia, respiratory depression (slowed breathing), altered gastrointestinal motility, euphoria (a "high feeling"), and **miosis** (contraction of the pupil). Codeine's cough suppressing action appears to involve binding between codeine itself (not its metabolite, morphine) and specific receptors in the cough center in the brain (see Chapter 2). This explains why morphine, which is so closely related to codeine chemically, has no effect on coughing and is never used as a cough suppressant.

The pain relieving, or analgesic, effects of codeine are similar to those of morphine, although much weaker in intensity. One of codeine's primary therapeutic uses is the treatment of mild-to-moderate pain, including post-operative pain, the acute "flare" of arthritis, and cancer pain. Codeine's analgesic **mechanism of action** occurs via the drug's conversion in the body from codeine (methylmorphine) to morphine. Codeine has an exceptionally low affinity for opioid receptors and it is the small fraction of codeine converted to morphine that is responsible for codeine's analgesic effect. Although a less potent painkiller than morphine, oral codeine is generally more potent than aspirin and other non-prescription "mild analgesics." A 30-mg oral dose of codeine provides the same pain relief as that achieved with 325 to 600 mg of aspirin. Interestingly, for many types of pain, aspirin and the so-called mild analgesics (specifically, the **nonsteroidal anti-inflammatory drugs**, or NSAIDs, such as ibuprofen) provide greater pain relief than the potent opioid analgesics if the pain is associated with inflammation. Classifying NSAIDs as mild analgesics is

Figure 3.6 Lock and key enzyme action. © Alfred Pasieka/Photo Researchers, Inc.

therefore inaccurate. Depending on the type of pain and the medical situation, aspirin and some NSAIDs can provide pain relief equivalent to 60 mg of oral codeine and 8 mg or more of parenteral (injected) morphine.

It is important to note that the binding of morphine to opioid receptors in the brain and spinal cord produces the *sensation* of pain relief; it does not attack or eliminate physical *causes* of pain due to trauma or other injury. At the cellular and molecular level, the binding of opioids with opioid receptors sets off a cascade of events that **modulate** the release of **neurotransmitters** involved in pain signaling.

How does codeine "know" what to do and where to go in the body? The answer lies with the distribution of opioid receptors throughout the body. The therapeutic effects of the opioids, including codeine, are indeed defined by their action on three specific types of opioid receptors in the body: delta (δ), mu (μ), and kappa (κ). (See Table 3.3.) The μ opioid receptors mediate most (but not all) of the actions of opioids: analgesia, euphoria, respiratory depression, miosis, and reduced gastrointestinal motility. The μ_1 opioid receptors, one subtype, are located in the

NATURAL HIGH:
Endorphins and Enkephalins

Endorphins and enkephalins are naturally occurring molecules that "ease the pain" when the body is in shock or under physically stressful conditions. Endorphins (*endo*genous, or naturally occurring within, as in within the body + m*orphine*) are secreted by the pituitary gland and have been identified in several areas of the brain, functioning to inhibit the perception of painful stimuli so that the body in essence feels no pain. Enkephalins (*enkephalos*, meaning within the head) are present in the spinal cord and, contrary to the Greek derivation of the work, in the peripheral nervous system (outside of the head). Interestingly, the discovery of these molecules in the 1970s is intimately related to research into the causes and effects of opium addiction. After identifying and characterizing receptors on the surface of nerve cells in the brain (neurons) that bind to opium and other opioids, researchers found previously unknown molecules synthesized in the brain could bind to these same receptors and, upon binding, produced the same analgesic, or pain-killing, effect as opioids. So, there's actually a biological basis to the euphoric sensation associated with high-level physical activity, such as the "runner's high" described by long-distance runners and exercise gurus: The euphoria is caused by the body's release of endorphins and enkephalins produced by prolonged exercise or stress on the body.

brain and mediate analgesia, whereas the μ_2 opioid receptors mediate respiratory depression. The analgesic effect of codeine, like that of morphine, occurs upon the binding of morphine to μ_1 opioid receptors to block pain signals. The δ opioid receptors also mediate analgesia, but are not considered as important as the μ opioid receptors for pain relief. In addition to analgesia,

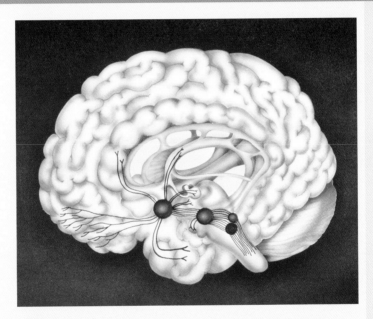

Figure 3.7 The binding sites and pathways (in red) of opiate (morphine-type) drugs. In the brainstem (rightmost two red spheres), sites involved in the transmission of pain include the nucleus raphe magnus and locus ceruleus, with other nuclei in the hypothalamus and thalamus (spheres to the left). Nerve pathways (red) extend to the frontal cortex (far left) and up into the limbic system (center-left). © Kairos, Latin Stock/Photo Researchers, Inc.

Table 3.3 **Select Therapeutic Effects Mediated by Opioid Receptors**

Effects	Opioid Receptor Type	
	μ, δ receptors	κ receptors
Analgesia	+++	+
Respiratory depression	++	+
Pupil constriction	+	-
Decreased gastrointestinal motility	++	-
Smooth muscle activity	++	-
Sedation	++	+
Euphoria	++	-
Dysphoria	-	+

- = no activity ; + = low activity; ++ = moderate activity; +++ = high activity

Source: H.B. Gutstein, and H. Akil. "Opioid analgesics" in *Goodman and Gilman's The Pharmacological Basis of Therapeutics.* 11th edition. Brunton, L.L; J.S. Lazo; K.L. Parker (eds). New York: McGraw-Hill, 2006.

the δ opioid receptors also mediate dysphoria (agitation or restlessness—the opposite of euphoria), hallucinations, and cough suppression.

With regard to analgesic effect, the average duration of action of the first single dose of codeine ranges from 1 to 6 hours, depending on the exact dose and route of administration—as explained above, it makes a difference whether the drug is swallowed or injected. (And the duration can vary considerably with multiple dosing.) For a 130-mg dose of intramuscularly administered codeine, the average duration of pain relief is one to two hours; for a 200-mg oral dose of codeine, the duration is four to six hours. Because it has a relatively short period of action, codeine is classified as a short-acting opioid analgesic. Morphine is also a short-acting (but more potent) opioid analgesic, with four to five hours of effectiveness.

Codeine's antitussive (cough-suppressing) action is unrelated to its analgesic effect, and is believed to occur through the direct action on the cough center in the medulla of the brain. The precise mechanism in humans, however, has not been clearly defined. It has been suggested that codeine suppresses the cough reflex via distinct receptors that bind to codeine itself, not morphine. Thus, unlike codeine's analgesic effect, which is due to the binding of morphine (the break-down product of codeine's metabolism) to opioid receptors, codeine's antitussive effect is due to unaltered codeine. Codeine is extremely effective in suppressing cough, and that is why, until similar-acting synthetic compounds were identified, it was a common ingredient in nonprescription cough preparations.

The next chapter addresses the unintended and unwanted side effects of or adverse reactions to codeine.

4

Toxicology

There are two sides to every drug: benefits and risks. In Chapter 2, we looked at codeine's benefits, or therapeutic effects—codeine as a painkiller, cough suppressant, and antidiarrheal agent. Codeine's risks, or side effects, are the unwanted, undesirable, unintended actions that can develop after codeine is ingested or injected. Studying the side effects of codeine is as important as studying the drug's therapeutic effects.

Toxicology, the study of toxic substances, is not just about poisons; the major focus of this branch of pharmacology is the **toxicity profile** of drugs (the complete array of side effects identified in experimental animals and humans following administration of one or more doses of a drug). Identifying and characterizing a drug's toxicities (the harmful side effects or adverse effects) is much like identifying and characterizing a drug's medicinal or therapeutic properties. Both aspects of drug action—safety *and* effectiveness— are important, and both aspects must be considered before a drug is allowed "on the market" (so it can be bought and sold) or before a drug is prescribed by a physician. (See FDA sidebar.)

In the case of an experimental drug, the process of seeking drug approval by the U.S. Food and Drug Administration (FDA) requires indisputable demonstration of the drug's safety. The best case scenario for an experimental drug, in addition to clear-cut demonstration of its effectiveness, would be that, after rigorous review, the FDA deems the drug safe with a favorable toxicity profile, meaning: The drug's side effects occur with low frequency (only a low percentage of treated patients actually experience a particular side effect), and

U.S. FOOD AND DRUG ADMINISTRATION (FDA) APPROVAL PROCESS FOR DRUGS

The FDA is the federal government agency whose directive is to ensure the safety and effectiveness of drugs. New drugs that are discovered and tested by pharmaceutical companies, government or private biomedical research organizations, or universities or academic medical centers must undergo formal evaluation by the FDA. The review process lasts about seven years on average. According to the FDA's Web site, "Most drugs that undergo preclinical (animal) testing never even make it to human testing and review by the FDA."

animal testing
▼
proposal for human testing in clinical trials
▼
Phase 1 clinical trials, to determine the drug's metabolism in the body and its most frequent side effects (typically involves 20 to 80 healthy individuals or "subjects")
▼
Phase 2 clinical trials, to obtain preliminary data on whether the drug works in individuals with the disease or condition targeted by the drug, the "target patient population" (typically involves at least 30 to about 300 individuals)
▼
Phase 3 clinical trials, to gather a larger set of data (typically involves several hundred to about 3,000 individuals)
▼
formal request by the "drug sponsor" for the FDA to consider a drug for marketing approval (the drug sponsor, usually a pharmaceutical company even if the drug was originally discovered in a university laboratory, files a new drug application)
▼
FDA scientists review the application to determine whether the studies the drug sponsor describe show that the drug is safe and effective for its proposed use.

Source: http://www.fda.gov/fdac/special/testtubetopatient/drugreview.html

PARACELSUS (1493–1541)

A Swiss-German physician and alchemist named Philippus Aureolus Theophrastus Bombastus Von Hohenheim, better known as Paracelsus, wrote about the two sides of drug action in an eloquent and memorable way: "All substances are poisons; there is none which is not a poison. The right dose differentiates a poison and a remedy."

PARACELSUS: Porträt nach der Ausg. der „Astronomica et Astrologica Opuscula", Köln 1567. Auf dem Schwertknauf das Wort „Zoth" (→ Azoth)

Figure 4.1 Engraved portrait of Paraclesus. © Stapleton Collection/CORBIS

the side effects identified during testing were mostly mild or moderate in intensity.

The undesirable side effects of a drug are either non-harmful or harmful. To identify any harmful side effects of a drug (adverse or toxic effects) in humans, toxicity studies are first conducted *in vitro* (usually in living cells that are maintained in petri dishes) and then in laboratory animals. These tests are most often conducted by the drug manufacturer and reviewed by the FDA. Knowing the toxic effects of a drug and the doses at which such effects occur allows for the safe use of the drug and, in the case of overdosage, successful management.

In the United States, the FDA requires toxicology tests before deeming a drug safe for use in humans. Animal toxicity tests are conducted in a variety of laboratory animals, which may include mice and rats, and if possible, "higher species" such as rabbits or dogs. Toxicology studies in several species allow researchers to look for species differences in response to different doses of the drug being studied; such information guides testing of the drug in humans. Nevertheless, one or more toxic effects may be unique to humans and may not have been observed in any animal tests. Animal testing also allows identification of toxicities that only occur at a specific age in life (e.g., newborns). Many drugs are not safe for use in newborns and infants because many of their body systems are not fully developed.

The initial "**preclinical**" assessment of a drug's potential toxicity is explored in mice or rats by identifying the lethal dosage (the dose that causes death in 50 percent of animals given the drug, designated **LD**$_{50}$). Although the LD$_{50}$ provides valuable information, the scientific method of observation can provide clues to the *mechanism* by which toxic effects arise. For example, direct observation can show whether the drug affects breathing or other biological functions.

If one or more side effects occur soon after a drug is given, they are referred to as acute or short-term toxicities.

Alternatively, side effects may not emerge until after repeated or prolonged exposure to the drug; these are called chronic or long-term toxicities. Studies evaluating acute toxicity are conducted over a few weeks, whereas those evaluating chronic toxicity are conducted from six months to one year.

Additional toxicology tests that are performed routinely evaluate liver and kidney function and effects on different blood components. Other studies are specially designed to assess whether exposure to a specific drug is associated with any effects on a developing embryo or fetus (teratogenic effects) or whether the drug causes cancer (**carcinogenic effects**). **Teratology** studies are conducted in pregnant animals to ensure that a drug is safe for the pregnant woman taking the drug and her fetus. Similarly, toxicity tests are carried out in female animals nursing their young to ensure that a drug is safe for lactating women and infants being nursed.

How a particular drug is metabolized, or broken down in the body, can affect its toxicity. Either the parent drug or one or more of its metabolites (break-down products) may be responsible for causing a particular toxic effect. As discussed in Chapter 3, codeine is metabolized to morphine by enzymes in the liver. The formation of a metabolite from a parent compound can be altered by one or more other drugs taken at the same time; the other drug(s) can interfere with the activity of metabolizing enzymes and thereby either speed up or slow down drug metabolism. Slowing down drug metabolism can mean that the drug "hangs around" in the body for a longer time, providing greater opportunity for the drug to cause damage. There is actually a list of drugs that, when given with codeine, can alter codeine's metabolism and can affect its toxicity (see "Drugs that Interact with Codeine" sidebar).

CODEINE'S SIDE EFFECTS

The spectrum of codeine's unwanted effects is listed in the Side Effects sidebar. Many of codeine's side effects are an extension

PHYSICIAN, DO NO HARM

Often medical practitioners are faced with weighing the benefits and risks of a treatment for their patient. Depending on the health status and age of the patient and the circumstances, the treatment—or, more accurately, the side effects of the treatment—can sometimes be worse than the ailment that is causing the suffering. When recommending a treatment plan for a patient, physicians are guided by a rule in the Hippocratic Oath that they take on becoming physicians "to do no harm" to those they are trying to heal. Hippocrates (c. 460–377 B.C.), the Greek physician and author of numerous texts on science and medicine, wrote in his book *Epidemics*, what is often referred to as the Hippocratic Oath: "As to diseases make a habit of two things—to help, or at least, to do no harm."

Figure 4.2 Illustration showing teaching of the aphorisms of Hippocrates. © J. L. Charmet/Photo Researchers, Inc.

of the drug's therapeutic effects: codeine's action on the central nervous system (to relieve pain, suppress cough) and gastrointestinal system (harden stool) can result in such side effects as drowsiness, mood alteration, and constipation. Not all of codeine's side effects are related to these body systems, however; some occur via codeine's action on the cardiovascular system, urinary tract, and smooth muscle of the bronchi (airways) of the lungs. Although it is an analgesic, codeine can actually cause pain in the stomach or abdomen by inducing spasms that increase pressure in the biliary tract (the system of ducts or vessels that carry bile from the liver where it is secreted to help digest metabolites to the gall bladder and other "downstream" organs for excretion).

An uncommon side effect of codeine is an allergic reaction, such as a skin rash or contact **dermatitis,** which is seen when codeine is administered by injection. **Delirium** is a rare side effect of codeine.

With repeated use of codeine, chronic toxicity can develop in the form of **tolerance,** physical **dependence,** and/or addiction. Tolerance is the loss of effectiveness associated with a specific drug dose over time, such that an increase in dose is required to produce the same effect. Dependence is a complex phenomenon in which repeated exposure to a drug results in a disturbance of the body's homeostatic mechanism (equilibrium or natural balance), which may only be revealed when the drug is abruptly stopped and symptoms of drug withdrawal develop (e.g., flu symptoms, restlessness, fever, chills, runny nose, or aches and pains). Tolerance and dependence are **physiological responses** that can develop in any patient exposed to a particular drug for a prolonged period. Addiction is a behavioral pattern characterized by compulsive use of a drug and fixation on obtaining more of the drug for personal use. Tolerance, dependence, and addiction are discussed in more detail in Chapter 5.

DRUG INTERACTIONS

Some undesirable effects can result from administering codeine and another drug at or about the same time (giving more than one drug at once is known as co-administration). Pharmacologists and toxicologists have figured out why the simultaneous use of two drugs can cause codeine to be a less effective pain reliever than it normally is: It has to do with the way the two drugs are metabolized in the body. Codeine's metabolism to morphine is largely mediated by the cytochrome P450 enzyme, CYP2D6. (Recall from Chapter 3 that codeine's chemical name is methylmorphine. You might want to go back to Chapter 3 to refresh your memory about the cytochrome P450 enzymes that are responsible for the metabolism of many drugs.) Fluoxetine (Prozac®), which inhibits the metabolic activity of CYP2D6, prevents much of codeine from being metabolized to morphine, and consequently, very little pain relief is afforded. The "Drugs that Interact with Codeine" sidebar lists a number of drug categories, technically known as *classes*, that are known to interfere with the CYP2D6 enzyme and that, when taken with codeine, either cause an adverse

KILLER ADVERSE DRUG REACTIONS

Some side effects, or adverse effects, of drugs can be fatal. Adverse drug reactions are one of the top 10 causes of death in hospitalized patients in the United States—as many as 100,000 deaths per year! Even aspirin at low doses, recommended to prevent heart attacks and stroke, can kill under the "right" conditions: Fatal bleeding can occur in patients who have an undetected clotting disorder and take aspirin regularly.

Source: J. Lazarou; B.H. Pomeranz; and P.N. Corey. "Incidence of adverse drug reactions in hospitalized patients: a meta-analysis of prospective studies," *Journal of the American Medical Association* 279 (1998): 1200–1205.

reaction or reduce or increase codeine's therapeutic effects. Several drugs, when given together with codeine, can enhance or exaggerate codeine's depressant effects on the central nervous system (increased **sedation** and decreased respiration). This can result in a serious adverse reaction requiring medical attention. With the exception of procarbazine, amphetamines, and quinidine, all of the agents and classes listed in the sidebar produce sedation and, when given together with codeine, increase the sedative effect of codeine. In contrast, ampheta-

COMMON SIDE EFFECTS OF CODEINE

ACUTE TOXICITIES

- Drowsiness (sedation)
- Nausea
- Pinpoint pupils (miosis)
- Mental clouding or mood alteration
- Vomiting
- Itching (pruritus)
- Dizziness
- Agitation or restlessness (dysphoria)
- Low blood pressure (hypotension)
- Urinary retention
- Respiratory depression
- Constipation

CHRONIC TOXICITIES

- Tolerance
- Physical dependence

Source: Gutstein, H.B., and H. Akil. "Opioid analgesics" in *Goodman and Gilman's The Pharmacological Basis of Therapeutics.* 11th edition. Brunton, LL; J.S. Lazo; K.L. Parker (eds). New York: McGraw-Hill, 2006.

mines may increase the analgesic effect and feeling of euphoria produced by codeine, while decreasing codeine's sedative effect. The muscle relaxant methocarbamol can increase the analgesic effect of codeine. Although it is not fully understood how these additive effects are produced, changes in codeine metabolism are believed to be involved.

VARIABLE METABOLISM OF CODEINE

Our understanding of drug-related toxicology has increased immensely with the recent explosion of advances in human genomics, in which human genes are deciphered and the linear sequence of deoxyribonucleic acid (DNA) revealed. (See Chapter 3 or the glossary for definitions of the terms *genomics*, *genes*, and *DNA*.) We now know that the enzymes involved in drug metabolism can vary from person to person, so that one

DRUGS THAT INTERACT WITH CODEINE

- other opioids (e.g., morphine)
- anesthetics
- phenothiazines (antipsychotics)
- barbiturates
- sedative/hypnotics
- chloral hydrate
- alcohol
- glutethimide

- amphetamines
- procarbazine HCl
- quinidine (antiarrhythmics)
- pyrazolidone antihistamines
- methocarbamol (muscle relaxant)
- ß (beta) blockers
- selective serotonin reuptake inhibitors (antidepressants)

Source: T.A. Ketter; D.A. Flockhart; R.M. Post; et al. "The emerging role of cytochrome P450 3A in psychopharmacology," *Journal of Clinical Psychopharmacology* 15 (1995): 387–398.

person's drug metabolizing enzymes can work more or less efficiently than another person's, which explains why some people do not respond to a particular drug in the same way as other people, even though they are given the same dose. Furthermore, some people may experience several of a particular drug's side effects while others don't experience any; likewise, some may experience severe side effects, while others experience only mild side effects. These findings have spawned several new specialties in pharmacology: pharmacogenetics, pharmacogenomics, and toxicogenomics.

As discussed in Chapter 3, codeine (methylmorphine) is primarily metabolized to morphine in the liver by the cytochrome P450 enzyme, CYP2D6. Like many drug-metabolizing enzymes in the cytochrome P450 superfamily, CYP2D6 can be dysfunctional or inactive due to a variation in the gene that encodes this enzyme. The variation in the CYP2D6 gene is not considered a mutation because that implies an error; rather, the variation is akin to the differences seen in such traits as hair and skin color. People with dysfunctional or inactive CYP2D6 enzymes are considered "poor metabolizers" with respect to codeine and other drugs that depend on CYP2D6 enzymes for their metabolism. (On the other end of the spectrum are people who are "ultrarapid extensive metabolizers," and in between are the "intermediate metabolizers" and "extensive metabolizers.")

People who are CYP2D6 poor metabolizers not only have a blunted response to codeine's pain-killing and other therapeutic effects, but they also are more likely to experience one or more of codeine's side effects and possibly to a greater degree than most people. Why? Because if codeine is poorly metabolized, then it remains in the body for a longer time, increasing the opportunity for adverse reactions to occur. People who are CYP2D6 poor metabolizers appear to experience the sedative effect of codeine more than others.

CODEINE POISONING / OVERDOSE

Codeine poisoning or an overdose of codeine may be accidental or intentional. Within one hour of ingestion of a large overdose of codeine, there is depression of the central nervous system: the patient may be in a stupor or may go into a coma.

PERSONALIZED MEDICINE: ONE DOSE DOES *NOT* FIT ALL

Toxicogenomics, like pharmacogenomics, examines an individual's genes to predict their response to a given drug. However, toxicogenomics is devoted to predicting an individual's *negative* response to a drug—that is, whether or not the individual will experience particular side effects of a drug. In the not-too-distant future, patients will be able to have a genetic test performed to identify the variant of the gene that encodes a drug-metabolizing (CYP) enzyme. This information will allow doctors to know how a particular patient will react to a particular drug at a particular dose, rather than hazard a guess based on the population average, which is the way medicine has been practiced for centuries. While experience tells us that everyone's body or "system" is different and that not everyone reacts the same to a particular drug, only recently has science been able to explain why: It's a matter of the genetics behind a body's drug metabolism. The recent advances in toxicogenomics mean:

- Individuals who require less medication than the standard dose of a drug will no longer be overmedicated and therefore will not be exposed to drug doses that could produce adverse events.

- Individuals who can only derive minimal, if any, benefit from a drug will no longer be given a prescription for that drug and therefore they will not be put at unnecessary risk of an adverse event.

CODEINE POISONING: A CASE STUDY

A 62-year-old white man with leukemia came into the Emergency Room after three days of feeling fatigued with shortness of breath, having a fever, and a cough. He had received cancer chemotherapy, which suppresses the immune system and leaves the body vulnerable to infections. The patient's medication history only included a daily dose of a preventive medicine for seizures (the patient only had one seizure several years earlier). On arrival to the ER, the patient was mentally alert. He was hypoxemic (low oxygen). Clinical evaluation and x-rays showed pneumonia in both lungs, and antibiotic therapy was started. Oral codeine was prescribed to relieve the cough (25 mg, every 8 hours).

On day 4, the patient began to lose consciousness and he became unresponsive. His last dose of codeine was 12 hours earlier. The patient was hypoxemic and was ventilated to improve his oxygen tissue levels. Clinical examination revealed pinpoint pupils, no eye opening, and no verbal response. Blood levels showed normal concentrations of the seizure medicine. The opioid antagonist naloxone was given twice, and each time the patient had dramatic improvement in his level of consciousness. Continued naloxone reversed the respiratory failure and the patient fully recovered after two days.

The signs and symptoms of codeine poisoning were recognized and treated appropriately. But what precipitated the patient's adverse reaction to oral codeine? The hospital ran some tests on the patient's blood taken at the time of his loss of consciousness and found that he had extremely high concentrations of codeine. Genetic testing was done and duplication in the gene that codes for the CYP2D6 enzyme was identified. The extra copies of this gene resulted in "ultrarapid metabolism" of codeine, which led to an increase in the conversion of codeine to morphine by the liver (hepatic CYP2D6 enzyme).

Source: Y. Gasche; Y. Daali; M. Fathi; A. Chiappe; S. Cottini; P. Dayer; and J. Desmeules. "Codeine intoxication associated with ultrarapid CYP2D6 metabolism," *New England Journal of Medicine* 351 (2004): 2827–2841.

Other signs of recent codeine overdosing are slowed breathing, hypoxia (low oxygen to the body's tissues), pinpoint pupils, and a decrease in body temperature with progressively falling blood pressure. Within four hours of an overdose and no treatment, severe respiratory depression progresses to coma. The resulting hypoxia due to the very low respiratory rate may lead to shock and finally respiratory failure, ending in death.

The successful management of codeine overdose consists of general life support measures such as assisted ventilation, administration of intravenous fluids, and **vasopressors**. When overdose is by ingestion (swallowing), evacuation of the stomach (gastric lavage) is sometimes performed to remove unabsorbed drug. In addition, **activated charcoal** may be administered to reduce absorption. Treatment with naloxone, an opiate **antagonist**, by intravenous injection, is sometimes used to treat overdosage of codeine or other opioids because of naloxone's ability to rapidly reverse severe respiratory depression.

5

Psychopharmacology

Drugs that affect the mind, or psyche (pronounced SIKE-ee), are referred to as **psychoactive** or **psychotropic** drugs. An extraordinary number of drugs affect the psyche (a word derived from the Greek *psyche* = life, soul), generally regarded as the organ of thought and judgment. **Psychopharmacology** is the study of drugs that affect the mind (conscious and unconscious mental processing) *and* behavior. Another term for psychoactive drugs is *centrally acting drugs,* referring to the action of these drugs on the central nervous system, which is composed of the brain and spinal cord. Codeine, morphine, and all the opioids are considered psychoactive drugs.

Psychoactive drugs can be classified by their chemical structure, clinical use, or according to their main behavioral effect as shown in Table 5.1. Codeine and other opiates are assigned to a category of their own due to the long medical and social history of opium-derived drugs. Although codeine is used therapeutically as a medicine to treat cough, pain, and diarrhea (see Chapter 2), one of its side effects is euphoria, which is defined as "an exaggerated feeling of physical and mental well-being." Depending on the dose and frequency of use, all opiates have this feel-good effect. It is the behavioral or mind-altering effect of codeine that makes the drug sought after by the codeine abuser.

DRUG ACTION

Each class of psychoactive substance exerts its effect through a unique mechanism of action. As a result, each class has certain unique features such as the behavioral effects they elicit, the rates at

Table 5.1 Select Therapeutic Effects Mediated by Opioid Receptors

Categories	Drug and "Substance" Examples
Sedatives (also called hypnotics, sedative-hypnotics, minor tranquilizers, antianxiety agents)	Secobarbital (barbiturate) Glutethimide (nonbarbiturate hypnotic) Diazepam (benzodiazepine antianxiety agent) Chloral hydrate (miscellaneous hypnotic) alcohol ("substance")
Stimulants	Dextroamphetamine (amphetamine) Caffeine ("substance")
Opiates	Codeine, morphine, heroin
Antipsychotic agents	Chlorpromazine (phenothiazine) Haloperidol (butyrophenone)
Psychedelics (also called hallucinogens)	LSD (lysergic acid diethylamide) ketamine marijuana

Source: Gutstein, H.B., and H. Akil. "Opioid analgesics" in *Goodman and Gilman's The Pharmacological Basis of Therapeutics*. 11th edition. Brunton, L.L.; J.S. Lazo; and K.L. Parker (eds). New York: McGraw-Hill, 2006.

which tolerance and dependence develop (see Substance Abuse Terminology sidebar). Researchers have found that the rates for tolerance and dependence are related to the types of receptors, or "receiving molecules" on the surface of cells, to which the drug binds in order to exert its effect on the cell. For example, tolerance and physical dependence to an opiate like codeine, which acts by binding to the μ and δ receptors, develops rapidly; however, tolerance to a sedative like diazepam, which acts on gamma-amino butyric acid (GABA) receptors, develops slowly. The withdrawal symptoms for the different categories of psychoactive drugs may also differ. For codeine and the opiates, withdrawal symptoms are similar to those of the flu, and include runny nose, fever, and the chills. For diazepam and other benzodiazepine antianxiety drugs, withdrawal symptoms include dizziness, increased sensitivity to light and sound, or sleep disturbances. Some of the benzodiazepine drugs have withdrawal symptoms that are cast as a "hangover" feeling.

All psychoactive substances share similarities in the way they alter the mind and the way they induce a "drug-rewarding system" (motivation and reward for continued use of the drug). All psychoactive substances affect a part of the brain called the midbrain, the location of two key areas involved in motivation and reinforcement. One of the midbrain areas, the *ventral tegmental area,* sends signals to regions of the brain involved in emotions, thoughts, memories, and planning and executing behaviors. The other midbrain area is the *nucleus accumbens,* which is involved in motivation and learning. It should be noted that for codeine and the opiates, the brain pathways involved in analgesia (pain relief) are distinct from those that control motivation and reinforcement.

POTENTIAL FOR ABUSE

Chronic use of codeine leads to tolerance. After repeated use of codeine, a particular dose loses its effect so that a higher dose is needed to provide the desired effect (such as relief from pain or coughing) that a smaller dose originally provided. This loss of sensitivity to a given dose of codeine is known as tolerance. Eventually, tolerance even develops to the euphoric effect ("high") of codeine, so that the euphoria becomes less intense over time. A patient may also develop a tolerance to some of codeine's other effects, both medicinal and toxic; for example, tolerance develops to codeine's analgesic and sedative effects, but not to its constipating (antidiarrheal) effect.

A consequence of tolerance is physical dependence, which occurs with long-term use. Physical dependence is the body's adaptation to the prolonged or continuous presence of codeine in its system. Both tolerance and dependence are closely related biological responses. In laboratory animal models of repeated drug use, the development of tolerance of and dependence on the opiate morphine appear to be closely linked. Substances that block tolerance, including chemical

SUBSTANCE ABUSE TERMINOLOGY

- Tolerance to a drug refers to the loss of effectiveness associated with a specific dose over time: After repeated or chronic use of a specific drug, an increase in dose is required to produce the same effect that a smaller dose produced originally. Tolerance is a biological phenomenon that can develop in any patient exposed to a particular drug for a prolonged period.

- Dependence on a drug is a physical or biological dependence involving the disturbance of the body's natural balance (equilibrium or homeostatic mechanism) due to repeated or chronic exposure to a drug. The disturbance may only be evident when the drug is abruptly stopped and symptoms of drug withdrawal develop, such as restlessness, flu symptoms, fever, chills, runny nose, and aches and pains. Dependence is a biological phenomenon that can develop in any patient exposed to a particular drug for a prolonged period.

- Addiction is a set of behaviors characterized by compulsive use of a drug and compulsion to obtain more of the drug for personal use. Psychological dependence, the intense craving or desire to repeatedly use a drug or obtain a drug because it produces a sense of improved well-being, is a component of addictive behavior.

signaling molecules called *neurotransmitters*, are also effective in blocking dependence. The development of both tolerance and physical dependence contributes to codeine's potential for addiction. Psychological dependence, a component of addictive behavior, refers to ideation about a drug and the intense desire to obtain and repeatedly use a drug.

Physical dependence is actually defined by what happens when a substance is taken away (withdrawn). Thus, dependence is characterized by the development of an assortment of *withdrawal symptoms*. A person who develops dependence on a drug needs the drug to function normally. Codeine dependence develops when the use of codeine is stopped abruptly. Withdrawal symptoms are generally unique to the individual classes of psychoactive drugs and are the body's response to the removal of a drug. Withdrawal is how the body reacts to its new state of not having the drug in its system. The brain and the rest of the body must adapt to the drug's absence. The withdrawal symptoms of codeine are similar to those seen with morphine, but milder. The milder symptoms are explained by codeine pharmacology: Recall that the active metabolite (break-down product) of codeine is morphine. Not all of codeine is metabolized to morphine, and therefore the binding of codeine's metabolite (morphine) with the opioid receptors that mediate codeine's effects is less than that of pure morphine. The withdrawal symptoms seen are similar to flu symptoms and include restlessness, sweating, runny nose, fever, chills, aches and pains, and vomiting. While codeine's withdrawal symptoms are uncomfortable and can feel unbearable, they are rarely life-threatening.

Addiction is a complex behavior that refers to compulsive drug use. Addiction research is one of the few scientific areas that involves the biological and social sciences: neurobiology, psychology, and sociology. Because of its complexity, there is much disagreement on the precise medical definition of addiction. It is sometimes (confusingly) called *drug dependence* or *psychological dependence.*

Many factors influence a person's risk for developing addiction to a substance, such as drugs, alcohol, or cigarettes. Nevertheless, the substance-seeking behavior and use of the substance becomes *the* priority in the person's life. A key feature of addiction is the person's knowledge of and fear of the physical symptoms of withdrawal; however, addiction is clearly different from tolerance and physical dependence. According to the results of a survey conducted in 2004 by the Substance Abuse and Mental Health Administration, one of the federal agencies that studies addiction, more than 6 million people aged 12 and older reported using codeine for nonmedical (recreational) reasons. The ready availability of codeine without a prescription (from online pharmacies) as well as of over-the-counter codeine-containing medicines facilitates the prevalence of codeine abuse.

As mentioned in Chapter 2, codeine is available in different formulations (tablets, liquids) and different milligram (mg) strengths. The higher codeine doses are regulated; a prescription is required for higher doses because of the greater potential for abuse with chronic use. In the United States, the Controlled Substances Act dictates how codeine is sold, whether by prescription only or over-the-counter. Codeine is more tightly controlled by federal and state regulations when it is combined with aspirin or acetaminophen or other drugs, either in tablets or as a cough syrup. (A further discussion of controlled substances and the legal issues of codeine follows in Chapter 6.)

In the United States and other countries, some cough syrups and tablets containing codeine are available without prescription, usually those with less than 10 mg of codeine. Houston, Texas, has been called the "city of syrup" because of the city's high rates of codeine abuse (see sidebar). In France, 95 percent of the consumption of a codeine-containing cough preparation called Néo-codion cannot be attributed to medical use alone. And in Thailand, until recently, the nonmedical use of codeine-containing cough syrup by teenagers was reported to be extensive. The potential for codeine abuse has led to the search for alternatives to codeine as well as more stringent sale of codeine-containing products.

"GETTING A CUP OF LEAN ON"

The Houston, Texas, hip-hop artist DJ Screw pioneered the slowed-down *screwed* and chopped sound of rap music. His music often consisted of odes to "getting a cup of lean on," referring to large cups of Kool-Aid and the codeine-containing cough syrup, promethazine. "Lean" and "syrup" are slang for these codeine-containing concoctions. DJ Screw (aka Robert Earl Davis Jr.) may have gained more notoriety for the way he died in 2000 than for his music. DJ Screw died from drug overdose, and codeine was one of several drugs noted as contributing to his death.

6

Controlled Substances

Narcotic is a legal term that refers to drugs associated with varying degrees of potential for abuse and addiction; but originally the term was used to describe drugs that induce sleep. *Narcotic* is derived from a Greek word meaning "to numb," as in to deaden or dull the senses. Before the term was applied globally to all drugs with a potential for abuse or addiction, *narcotic* was used exclusively to refer to opioids.

In 1970, the U.S. Congress passed the Controlled Substances Act as a means to regulate the manufacture, importation, possession, and distribution of psychoactive drugs (see Chapter 5). The rationale for the legislation was public safety. The Drug Enforcement Agency (DEA) is the government organization responsible for enforcing the provisions of the Controlled Substances Act. Enforcement includes the licensing of manufacturers of controlled drugs, setting the quotas for the manufacture of these drugs, and regulating pharmacies that dispense such drugs and the physicians, physician assistants, and nurse practitioners who prescribe the drugs. The Controlled Substances Act created five categories of controlled substances called "schedules," which are differentiated by the relative potential for abuse. Schedule I substances, for example, have the greatest potential for abuse and addiction, while schedule V substances have the least potential for abuse and addiction. (See sidebar.)

Figure 6.1 Agents of the Drug Enforcement Administration regulate controlled stubstances and fight their illegal distribution and use. © David Butow/CORBIS SABA.

As discussed in Chapter 2, the primary medical uses of codeine are for the relief of pain, cough suppression, and to control diarrhea. Codeine is commercially produced as tablets, either alone (Schedule II), in combination with aspirin or acetaminophen (Schedule III), or as a liquid preparation for suppressing cough suppressant (Schedule V).

In the U.S., all opioids are controlled substances. Section 802 of the Controlled Substances Act defines an opiate as:

> ... any drug or other substance having an addiction-forming or addiction-sustaining liability similar to morphine or being capable of conversion into a drug having such addiction-forming or addiction-sustaining liability.

"SCHEDULES" ESTABLISHED BY THE CONTROLLED SUBSTANCES ACT

SCHEDULE I

- The drug or substance has a high potential for abuse.

- The drug or substance has no currently accepted medical use in treatment in the United States (e.g., heroin, cocaine, LSD).

- There is a lack of accepted safety for use of the drug or other substance under medical supervision.

SCHEDULE II

- The drug or substance has a high potential for abuse.

- The drug or substance has a currently accepted medical use in the United States or has a currently accepted medical use with severe restrictions.

- Abuse of the drug or substance may lead to severe psychological or physical dependence.

* Codeine in tablet form, with no other analgesic compound, is a Schedule II drug.

SCHEDULE III

- The drug or other substance has a lower potential for abuse than the drugs or substances in schedules I and II

- The drug or substance has a currently accepted medical use in the United States.

- Abuse of the drug or substance may lead to moderate or low-level physical dependence or high-level psychological dependence.

* Codeine in tablet form in combination with aspirin or acetaminophen (e.g., Tylenol® with Codeine) is a Schedule III drug.

continued on page 72

continued from page 71

SCHEDULE IV

- The drug or substance has a low potential for abuse relative to the drugs or substances in schedule III.

- The drug or substance has a currently accepted medical use in the United States.

- Abuse of the drug or other substance may lead to limited physical dependence or psychological dependence relative to the drugs or other substances in schedule III.

SCHEDULE V

- The drug or substance has a low potential for abuse relative to the drugs or other substances in schedule IV.

- The drug or substance has a currently accepted medical use in treatment in the United States.

- Abuse of the drug or substance may lead to limited physical dependence or psychological dependence relative to the drugs or other substances in schedule IV.

* Codeine in liquid form for use as a cough suppressant (e.g., Robitussin A-C®, Cheracol®, Pediacof®) is a Schedule V drug.

Table 6.1 Penalties for Illegal Possession of a Controlled Substance*

DRUG/SCHEDULE	QUANTITY	PENALTIES
Schedule I and II drugs	Any amount	First Offense: Not more than 20 yrs in prison. If death or serious injury, not less than 20 yrs, or more than life. Fine: $1 million if an individual, $5 million if not an individual. Second Offense: Not more than 30 yrs. If death or serious injury, not less than life. Fine: $2 million if an individual, $10 million if not an individual.
Schedule III drugs	Any amount	First Offense: Not more than 5 yrs. Fine: not more than $250,000 if an individual, $1 million if not an individual. Second Offense: Not more than 10 yrs. Fine: Not more than $500,000 if an individual, $2 million if not an individual.
Schedule IV drugs	Any amount	First Offense: Not more than 3 yrs. Fine: not more than $250,000 if an individual, $1 million if not an individual. Second Offense: Not more than 6 yrs. Fine: Not more than $500,000 if an individual, $2 million if not an individual.

Table 6.1 continued

DRUG/SCHEDULE	QUANTITY	PENALTIES
Schedule V drugs	Any amount	First Offense: Not more than 1 yr. Fine: Not more than $100,000 if an individual, $250,000 if not an individual. Second Offense: Not more than 2 yrs. Fine: Not more than $200,000 if an individual, $500,000 if not an individual.

* Different penalties apply for cocaine, fentanyl, heroin, LSD, methamphetamine, PCP, flunitrazepam, marijuana, and hashish

Source: U.S. Drug Enforcement Agency. Available online at http://www.dea.gov.

According to the Controlled Substances Act, the term "narcotic drug" refers to more than just opiate drugs; it also includes opium, poppy straw, derivatives of opium and opiates, cocaine, coca leaves, and extracts that contain cocaine and ecgonine (the major metabolite of cocaine) and its derivatives. These may be directly or indirectly produced by extraction from substances, by chemical synthesis, or by a combination of both methods.

Determining the abuse potential of a drug is the responsibility of the U.S. Food and Drug Administration (FDA), which recommends to the DEA a specific schedule to assign a drug with abuse potential. The abuse potential of a drug is evaluated during the preclinical and clinical phases of the drug development process before the drug becomes commercially available. While the potential for abuse is a major criterion in determining a drug's schedule, its medical use and the strength of the dependence that the drug can induce are also important criteria. Doctors, physician assistants, and nurse practitioners who write prescriptions for patients know the schedule for every drug. They must report all prescriptions they write for Schedule II drugs—it's the "controlled" part of "controlled substances." Prescriptions do not exist for Schedule I substances (those with the greatest potential for abuse and addiction) because this category is reserved for drugs with no medical use and cannot be possessed legally. Illegal possession of a controlled substance carries stiff penalties (see sidebar).

7

Complementary and Alternative Medicine

Not everyone is enamored with pharmacology, clinical science, or medicine. In fact, there's a growing proportion of the population that is interested in nontraditional or non-Western medical approaches to health and healing—commonly referred to as *alternative* or *complementary medicine*. (Actually, "nontraditional medicine" is a misnomer: In reality, such remedies as herbs, aromatherapy, and Chinese acupuncture can usually be traced to their use among generations and generations of cultures, where it was and maybe still is *tradition* to use a particular remedy for a particular condition.) "Alternative medicine" is now understood to refer to health practices that are an alternative to conventional Western medicine or pharmaceutical-grade drugs. "Complementary" refers to the use of non-Western health approaches, such as acupuncture, chiropractic, or aromatherapy, for example, *in addition to* (to complement) conventional Western medicine.

There is an evolving variety of alternative healthcare practices and products to choose from. (See Terminology sidebar.) Adults and adolescents alike are asking themselves questions such as, "Should I take a pill for my headache, or drink chamomile herbal tea?" There are several scientific counterparts to this seemingly simple question, for example: Are these both remedies? Are they equally effective? Is one healthier or less toxic than the other? Can they be used together? At this time, there is no comparative information on codeine versus alternative medicine (e.g., acupuncture) as effective treatments for pain, cough, and diarrhea.

Because of the interest in and popularity of alternative and complementary medicines and healing practices, the scientific method is being applied to a wide variety of these remedies. Different types of studies seek to establish if and how individual, alternative medicines exert their effect. Clinical trials are being conducted to compare a specific alternative medicines with the accepted conventional medical standard of care for a specific condition; thus, for example, an herbal extract may be compared with a pharmaceutical-grade drug to demonstrate unequivocally the safety and effectiveness of a product or practice. However, complementary and alternative medicine has only recently been deemed worthy of scientific scrutiny (for decades many natural remedies and practices were dismissed outright as being "obviously inferior" to Western science–based medicine), and many alternative therapies have not yet been

(*continued on page 81*)

Figure 7.1 Small baskets of Ayurvedic medicine, a traditional Sri Lankan medical practice. © Lindsay Hebberd/CORBIS

COMPLEMENTARY AND ALTERNATIVE MEDICINE TERMINOLOGY

- Acupuncture is a method of healing developed in China at least 2000 years ago. Today, acupuncture encompasses a family of procedures involving stimulation of anatomical points on the body by a variety of techniques. American practices of acupuncture incorporate medical traditions from China, Japan, Korea, and other countries. The acupuncture technique that has been most studied scientifically involves penetrating the skin with thin metallic needles that are manipulated by the hands or by electrical stimulation.

- Ayurveda has been practiced primarily in India for 5,000 years, and includes diet and herbal remedies and emphasizes the use of body, mind, and spirit in disease prevention and treatment.

- Chiropractic is a therapeutic approach rooted in the body's structure-function relationship. Chiropractors use manipulative therapy, primarily on the spine, joints, and muscles, to preserve and restore health.

- Dietary supplements are products taken by mouth that contain an ingredient intended to supplement the diet, such as vitamins, minerals, herbs or other botanicals, amino acids, and substances such as enzymes, organ tissues, and metabolites. Dietary supplements come in many forms, including extracts, concentrates, tablets, capsules, gel caps, liquids, and powders. They have special requirements for labeling. In the U.S., the Dietary Supplement Health and Education Act of 1994 states that dietary supplements are considered foods, not drugs. (Note that some dietary supplements are used in conventional medicine; for example, folic acid is given to pregnant women to prevent certain birth defects, and a regimen of vitamins and zinc can slow the progression of an eye disease called *age-related macular degeneration*.)

- Energy therapies are intended to affect energy fields that are said to surround and penetrate the human body. Some forms of energy therapy manipulate "biofields" by applying pressure and/or manipulating the body by placing the hands in, or through, these fields, such as Reiki and *qi gong*. Energy therapies also include the unconventional use of electromagnetic fields.

- Homeopathic medicine is built upon the belief that "like cures like," meaning that small, highly diluted quantities of medicinal substances can be given to cure symptoms and, conversely, the same substances given at higher or more concentrated doses cause those symptoms. Examples include traditional Chinese medicine.

- Mind-body medicine uses a variety of techniques designed to enhance the mind's capacity to affect bodily function and symptoms. Mind-body healing techniques include meditation, prayer, mental healing, and therapies that use creative outlets such as art, music, and dance.

- Naturopathic medicine, or naturopathy, proposes that there is a healing power *in the body* that establishes, maintains, and restores health. Practitioners work with the patient with a goal of supporting this power through treatments such as nutrition and lifestyle counseling, dietary supplements, medicinal plants, exercise, homeopathy, and treatments from traditional Chinese medicine.

• Traditional Chinese medicine is the modern name for the ancient art of healing that originated in China. Traditional Chinese medicine is based on a concept of balanced *Qi* (pronounced "chee"), or vital energy, that is believed to flow throughout the body. According to traditional Chinese medicine principles, Qi regulates a person's spiritual, emotional, mental, and physical balance and is influenced by the opposing forces of *yin* (negative energy) and *yang* (positive energy) that exist within each person. When yin and yang are imbalanced, disease occurs. Acupuncture and meditation are components of traditional Chinese medicine.

• Therapeutic massage is the manipulation of muscles and connective tissue to enhance function of those tissues and promote relaxation and well-being.

NCCAM

In the United States, the National Center of Complementary and Alternative Medicine (NCCAM) was created in 1998 as one of the many research institutes and centers within the prestigious National Institutes of Health (NIH). This government research center collaborates with academic medical centers to evaluate specific nontraditional approaches to health and healing by conducting clinical trials and other scientific studies, as is done for drugs.

(*continued from page 77*)

subjected to rigorous clinical testing, in which proof of effectiveness and safety must be demonstrated in a large sample of people. For this reason, health care professionals strongly warn patients to use caution with alternative therapies for which there are no definitive data. Table 7.1 provides a list of Internet sources for information on individual complementary and alternative medicines.

PAIN MANAGEMENT

The list of complementary and alternative medicines for analgesics is quite long and depends on how far and wide you look for the information. The following is a list of alternative therapies for pain relief, including therapies which have reliable scientific data to support their use as well as those being studied:

- Traditional Chinese medicine, particularly acupuncture

- Touch therapies and/or energy fields

- Chiropractic: for multiple sources of pain

- Weight reduction, exercise

- Hypnosis or hypnotherapy

- Amino acids: Scientific data show a substantial health benefit for D-phenylalanine as an analgesic.

- Dietary supplements: For migraines, scientific data show a substantial health benefit for magnesium and Vitamin B_2. Contradictory, insufficient, or preliminary studies suggest a health benefit or minimal health benefit for 5-HTP, Coenzyme Q10, and Vitamin B_{12}

- Herbal products: Scientific data show a substantial health benefit for the spice cayenne (topical capsaicin) as an analgesic and feverfew for migraine headaches. Contradictory, insufficient, or preliminary studies suggest a health

Table 7.1 **Federal Government Web Sites that Provide Information on Complementary and Alternative Medicine**

http://www.nccam.nih.gov	National Center for Complementary and Alternative Medicine (NCCAM) is part of the National Institutes of Health; the Center provides scientific information on complementary and alternative healing practices.
http://www.nccam.nih.gov/ clinicaltrials	NCCAM Web site for clinical trials conducted in humans to scientifically evaluate complementary or alternative therapies.
http://www.ods.od.nih.gov	Office of Dietary Supplements (ODS) directs the scientific study of dietary supplements.
http://www.ods.od.nih.gov/ databases/ibids.htm	ODS database of International Bibliographic Information on Dietary Supplements (IBIDS).
http://www.nlm.nih.gov	The National Library of Medicine, a part of the National Institutes of Health.
http://www.pubmed.gov	PubMed, short for medical publications, is the National Library of Medicine's database of scientific articles published in scientific journals. The database provides citations and abstracts of the journal articles.
http://www.nlm.nih.gov/nccam/ camonpubmed.html	"CAM on PubMed" is a subset of the PubMed database limited to complementary and alternative therapies.
http://dirline.nlm.nih.gov	The National Library of Medicine's directory of health organizations.
http://www.fda.gov	The U.S. Food and Drug Administration (FDA) is a scientific, regulatory, and public health agency that monitors food, drugs, medical devices, and cosmetics. This U.S. agency was essentially created in 1906 (with the Federal Food and Drugs Act) to safeguard the public against contaminated food as well as useless or toxic medicines.
http://www.cfsan.fda.gov	NIH/FDA database of federal and privately funded trials on human volunteers.

Table 7.1 **continued**

http://www.cfsan.fda.gov	Center for Food Safety and Applied Nutrition regulates and implements policy on safety of dietary supplements.
http://www.fda.gov/medwatch/report/consumer/consumer.htm	FDA program for reporting of serious adverse events or illness caused by drugs, medical devices, medical foods, and dietary supplements.
http://www.fda.gov/opacom/7alerts.html	FDA Web site for product recalls and safety alerts.
http://www.ftc.gov	Federal Trade Commission (FTC) provides information on fraudulent claims and therapy-related consumer alerts.
http://www.ftc.gov/bcp/menu-health.htm	FTC Web site for consumer information on diet, health, and fitness.

benefit or minimal health benefit for the alkaloid cory-dalis as an analgesic and Butterbur for migraines.

- Transcutaneous electric nerve stimulation (non-spinal cord) as a general analgesic; percutaneous electric nerve stimulation for migraine headaches

ANTITUSSIS

The following list of alternative therapies for suppressing cough is not exhaustive; it includes nontraditional remedies for which there are either reliable scientific data to support their use and those being studied:

- Traditional Chinese medicine, including acupuncture, herbal products for asthma and bronchitis

- Homeopathy: *Aconitum napellus*, Belladonna, Bryonia, Chamomilla, *Ferrum phosphoricum, Hepar sulphuris calcareum, Ipecacuanha, Nux vomica,* Phosphorus, Pulsatilla, *Rumex crispus, Spongia tosta,* Sulphur

ANTIDIARRHEAL

The following is a list of alternative therapies for diarrhea; it includes dietary supplements and herbal products for which there are either reliable scientific data to support their use or those being studied:

- Lactase for lactose-intolerant people

- Multiple vitamin-mineral

- Probiotic bacteria for infectious and antibiotic-associated diarrhea

- Brewer's yeast for infectious diarrhea

- Bovine colostrum

- Fiber, including Psyllium seed husks (a fiber source)

- Glutamine to promote the health of intestinal lining

- Carob (dried powdered pod)

- Tannin-containing products, such as teas, for their binding effect on mucus membranes

- Sangre de drago, a Peruvian herb (bark extract)

- Tormentil root extract, a European herb for rotavirus infection

absorption—In pharmacology, the uptake of drugs or substances into or across tissues, such as absorption of an orally administered drug into the bloodstream.

activated charcoal—Highly absorptive charred wood used as a general purpose antidote, especially in hospital emergency rooms for drug overdoses.

addiction—A set of behaviors characterized by compulsive use of a psychoactive (mind-altering) drug or substance and a compulsion to obtain more drug or substance for personal use.

affinity—Chemical or electrostatic attraction; in pharmacology, the attraction can also be defined as the tightness of the fit between a drug and a receptor on a cell surface.

alkaloid—A nitrogen-containing compound.

amygdala—An area of the cerebrum of the brain responsible for emotions, including responses to threatening environmental stimuli.

analgesia—Relief from pain; an analgesic is a drug or substance that reduces pain.

antagonist—A drug that blocks the activity of a molecule, including a receptor molecule; receptor antagonists interfere with the binding of a molecule to the receptor thereby thwarting the normal biological response to such binding (e.g., pain relief).

antiarrhythmic—A drug that regulates beating of the heart.

antibiotic—A drug that inhibits the growth of or kills bacteria (one type of disease-causing microorganisms); antibiotics are not effective against viruses, another type of disease-causing microorganism.

antihistamine—A drug that reduces itching, swelling, and mucous secretions.

antipyretic—A drug that relieves or reduces fever.

antitussive—A drug that relieves or prevents cough.

barbiturate—Class of drugs having sedative and/or hypnotic effects.

biliary tract—Body system comprised of the gallbladder, bile ducts, and bile.

blood components—Plasma, red blood cells, white blood cells, and platelets.

bronchi—Larger air passages of the lung.

bronchodilator—Drug that causes expansion of the air passages of the lungs.

carcinogenic effect—To cause cancer; the carcinogenic effects of some drugs may not be apparent until after long-term repeated use.

cardiovascular system—The heart and blood vessels.

carotid artery—Main artery leading to the head.

central nervous system—Brain and spinal cord.

Glossary

cerebrum—The largest part of the vertebrate brain responsible for processing complex sensory information (higher thinking) and controlling voluntary muscle activity.

chemotherapy—Treatment of disease with chemicals or drugs; generally used in relation to cancer when unqualified, but it is correct to use when not referring to cancer (e.g., antimicrobial chemotherapy).

clearance—Rate of removal of a substance from an organ or body.

coma—State of prolonged unconsciousness.

constipation—Infrequent or difficult elimination of feces, as sometimes caused by high doses or too frequent dosing of codeine when used for cough or pain.

cyanosis—Bluish discoloration of skin from inadequate oxygen retention in the blood.

cytochrome P450 system—The family of enzymes that are responsible for the metabolism of some foods and many commonly used drugs, including codeine.

defecation—Elimination of feces from the body.

delirium—An acute, reversible condition of disorganized thinking.

demethylation—Removal of a methyl group ($-CH_3$) from a compound; codeine's metabolism in the body includes the demethylation of codeine to form morphine.

deoxyribonucleic acid (DNA)—A large molecule that is the basic genetic material of all organisms.

dependence—Unless qualified, a physical or biological response reflecting a disturbance of the body's natural balance (equilibrium or homeostatic mechanism) due to repeated or chronic exposure to a drug; psychological dependence, distinct from physical dependence, is a component of addictive behavior.

dermatitis—Inflammation of the skin.

dysfunctional—Inability to function properly; can apply to molecules (e.g., proteins), cells, organs, organisms.

dysphoria—Agitation, restlessness, disquiet.

electroencephalograph—Measurement of electrical signaling by the brain.

endorphins—A family of peptide molecules (protein fragments) belonging to the endogenous opioid system; endorphins bind to opioid receptors during long periods of physical exercise or under other stressful conditions, thereby producing a pleasant feel-good sensation or potent analgesic effect.

enkephalins—A family of peptide molecules (protein fragments) belonging to the endogenous opioid system; like their relatives, the endorphins and dynorphins, enkephalins produce a euphoric sensation upon binding to opioid receptors in the body.

enzyme—A protein molecule that facilitates a chemical reaction without being changed itself; enzymes can speed up or slow down chemical reactions in the body, including the metabolism of drugs.

euphoria—An exaggerated feeling of well-being.

excretion—Elimination of waste.

expectorant—Drug that promotes ejection of mucus from airway passages.

formulation—The form of drug when it is ready to be used, such as tablet, capsule, or syrup.

gastrointestinal—Relating to the stomach and intestines.

gene—A discrete DNA (deoxyribonucleic acid) segment that contains all the necessary information for making a specific product, such as a protein; genetics is the study of genes and heredity.

genome—The complete set of an organism's genes or genetic material; genomics is the study of the genome of a species (e.g., humans) or an individual member of a species.

half-life—The time required for half of the amount of a substance or drug to degrade or be eliminated.

hemoglobin—Oxygen-carrying pigment of red blood cells.

hepatic—Pertaining to the liver.

hepatitis C virus—A virus that infects the liver, causing progressive damage to this organ; the virus is transmitted by transfusion or transplantation of hepatitis C virus-contaminated blood or organ, by the sharing of contaminated needles or syringes.

homeostatic mechanism—Biological process contributing to the normal stability, or equilibrium, of the body.

hypoxia—Low oxygen in body tissues despite adequate blood flow.

in vitro—Within a test tube or other artificial environment.

in vivo—Within the living body.

ionization—Process whereby a neutral atom gains an electrical charge.

lactation—The secretion of milk.

LD_{50}—The dosage level of a drug that is strong enough to cause death in 50 percent of animals tested; referred to as 50 percent lethal dose.

liquid suspension—A drug formulation in which the active ingredient is carried (suspended), but not dissolved, in a fluid.

Glossary

magnetic resonance imaging (MRI)—Creating images using a magnetic field and radio waves so that internal body parts can be visualized.

mechanism of action—In pharmacology, the exact process by which a drug exerts its effect; codeine's mechanism of action occurs through its binding with opioid receptors in the brain.

medicinal chemistry—Area of chemistry that pertains to drug therapy or healing.

medulla oblongata—Part of the brainstem that is continuous with the spinal cord, responsible for the involuntary actions of breathing and heart functioning.

metabolism—Biochemical transformation of a compound into changed, often smaller, molecules (metabolites, or the breakdown products of metabolism).

methylation—Replacement of a hydrogen atom for a methyl group.

methyl group—Three hydrogen atoms bonded to a single carbon atom, designated CH_3.

miosis—Contraction of the pupil, producing "pinpoint" pupils.

modulate—Adjust or alter an action, such as the speed, intensity, or functioning of the transmission of pain signals between neurons in the brain or some other biological process.

motility—Movement that is spontaneous, such as movement of the bowels.

motor—Affects motion or produces movement; in relation to the nervous system, motor functions or motor reflexes involve muscle.

mucus—Slippery secretion of moist membranes; mucous (related to mucus secretions) is the adjective form of mucus.

narcotic—Any drug or substance that produces a generalized depression of brain functioning, which manifests as insensibility or stupor. The term *narcotic* was originally a medical term and was restricted to opioids.

nausea—Unpleasant sensation that often precedes vomiting.

neurons—Nerve cells involved in the relaying of information to and from the brain and spinal cord.

neurotransmitters—Chemical substances released from neurons when an electrical impulse is received and which trigger an impulse in an adjacent neuron.

nonsteroidal anti-inflammatory drugs (NSAIDs)—Class of non-opioid analgesics.

opiate—Any drug derived from opium, including morphine, codeine, and papaverine.

opioid—Any natural or synthetic compound that acts like morphine or that binds to or influences opioid receptors; includes morphine, codeine, endorphins, enkephalins, heroin.

opium—The dried, milky juice obtained from the unripe capsules of the poppy plant, *Papaver somniferum*, and a source for morphine and codeine.

organic chemistry—Production and study of compounds that contain carbon.

parent drug, compound or molecule—Form of active ingredient prior to metabolic transformation.

parenteral—Any route of administration that excludes the gastrointestinal tract, thus avoiding degradation of medication sensitive to acid.

peptides—Protein fragments comprised of short sequences of amino acids.

peripheral nervous system—All parts of the nervous system except for the brain and spinal cord.

petri dish—Small, clear glass or plastic plate used in the laboratory for conducting *in vitro* experiments or studies.

pharmaceutical grade—High-quality, concentration form of a drug used to make formulations of medicine.

pharmaceutical science—Study of the preparation, administration, and development of drugs.

pharmacogenetics—Study of genetic factors and responses to drugs.

pharmacogenomics—Analysis of an individual's genes to predict response to a drug.

pharmacology—Study of drug action, including origin, effects, and uses of drugs.

phlegm—A ropy, thick mucous secretion produced in respiratory passages.

physiological response—Effect on the functioning of a living organism.

plasma—Fluid portion of the blood in which other components are suspended.

pneumonia—Lungs that are inflamed and filling with fluids.

potency—Drug dose needed to have a desired effect.

preclinical—Before evaluation in human volunteers.

receptors—Molecules on the surface of cells that, upon interaction or binding with specific molecules, trigger a set of cellular events that result in an effect such as pain relief; codeine binds with opioid receptors to produce its analgesic effect.

renal—Pertaining to the kidney.

respiratory airways—Air passages of the lungs.

Glossary

routes of delivery—Method by which a drug is administered, e.g., oral versus intravenous or intramuscular injection.

sedation—Production of a calming effect; a sedative alleviates excitement and produces calmness or sleepiness.

sensory—Relating to the senses (vision, hearing, smelling, tasting, feeling).

sickle cell anemia—A hereditary disease in which red blood cells are misshapen (they look like scythes).

smooth muscle—Muscles that act (contract and expand) involuntarily (without conscious thought); these include muscles surrounding the bladder, intestines, and blood vessels.

solubility—Ability of a substance or drug to be dissolved; in pharmacology, a drug's solubility is generally qualified as either *aqueous* (in water) or *lipid* (in fat-containing liquid) solubility.

stool—Feces.

stupor—Lowered level of consciousness.

symptomatic—Related to symptoms of disease or illness.

synthetic compounds—Chemicals produced by artificial means; many modern drugs are synthesized compounds, rather than natural products.

tannins—Compounds found in plants that have an astringent taste.

teratology—Study of abnormal development and congenital defects; teratogenic effects of a drug are those that cause physical or mental abnormalities in an embryo or fetus.

therapeutic—Beneficial or curative; *therapeutic* refers to a potentially beneficial treatment when it is distinguished from a preventive agent such as a vaccine.

tolerance—Decrease in drug effectiveness with repeated or prolonged use of drug.

toxicity profile—The complete array of harmful side effects identified in experimental animals and humans following administration of one or more doses of a drug.

toxicogenomics—Study of gene variation as related to occurrence of drug toxicities or side effects.

toxicology—Branch of pharmacology dealing in the study of toxic substances or poisons.

trachea—Windpipe, the single tube that ends at the divide of the bronchi.

urinary tract—Body system pertaining to the containment or secretion of urine.

variability—In genes, differences in the coded instructions that result in differences in the activity or functioning of the gene or the expression of the trait that the gene encodes; genetic variability of drug-metabolizing enzymes explains the phenomenon whereby different people respond differently to the same dose of a particular drug.

vasopressor—A compound that stimulates contraction of muscles surrounding arteries and capillaries.

Bibliography

Books

Beers, M.H., and R. Berkow (eds). *The Merck Manual of Diagnosis and Therapy.* 17th edition. Whitehouse Station, NJ: Merck Research Laboratories, 1999.

Eaton, D.L., and C.D. Klaassen. "Principles of toxicology." in *Casarett and Doull's Toxicology: The Basic Science of Poisons.* 6th edition. New York: McGraw-Hill, 2001.

Gutstein, H.B., and H. Akil. "Opioid analgesics." in *Goodman and Gilman's The Pharmacological Basis of Therapeutics.* 11th edition. New York: McGraw-Hill, 2006.

Klaassen, C.D. "Principles of toxicology and treatment of poisoning." in *Goodman and Gilman's The Pharmacological Basis of Therapeutics.* 11th edition. New York: McGraw-Hill, 2006.

Lide, D.R. (ed). *CRC Handbook of Chemistry and Physics.* 87th edition. Cleveland, OH: The Chemical Rubber Co., 2006.

Oates, J.A. "The science of drug therapy." in *Goodman and Gilman's The Pharmacological Basis of Therapeutics.* 11th edition. New York: McGraw-Hill, 2006.

O'Brien, C.P. "Drug addiction and drug abuse." in *Goodman and Gilman's The Pharmacological Basis of Therapeutics.* 11th edition. New York: McGraw-Hill, 2006.

Articles

Ashburn, M.A., and P.S. Staats. "Management of chronic pain," *Lancet* 353 (1999): 1865–1869.

Beeson, J.M. "The neurobiology of pain," *Lancet* 353 (1999): 1610–1615.

Gasche, Y.; Y. Daali; M. Fathi; A. Chiappe; S. Cottini; P. Dayer; and J. Desmeules. "Codeine intoxication associated with ultrarapid CYP2D6 metabolism," *New England Journal of Medicine* 351 (2004): 2827–2841.

Ketter, T.A.; D.A. Flockhart; R.M. Post; et al. "The emerging role of cytochrome P450 3A in psychopharmacology," *Journal of Clinical Psychopharmacology* 15 (1995): 387–398.

King, M.A.; M.A. McDonough; O.H. Drummer; and S.F. Berkovic. "Poppy tea and the baker's first seizure," *Lancet* 350 (1997): 716.

Loeser, J.D., and R. Melzack. "Pain: an overview," *Lancet* 353 (1999): 1607–1609.

Memelink, J. "Putting the opium in poppy to sleep," *Nature Biotechnology* 22 (2004): 1566–1567.

Meyer, U.A. "Pharmacogenetics and adverse drug reactions," *Lancet* 356 (2000): 1667–1671.

Michalets, E. L. "Update: Clinically significant cytochrome P–450 drug interactions," *Pharmacotherapy* 18 (1998): 84–112.

Nerbert, D.W., and D.W. Russell. "Clinical importance of the cytochromes P450," *Lancet* 360 (2002): 1155–1162.

Rodgers, J.F.; A.N. Nafziger; and J.S. Bertino. "Pharmacogenetics affects dosing, efficacy, and toxicity of cytochrome P450-metabolized drugs," *American Journal of Medicine* 113 (2002): 746–750.

Roth, S.H. "A new role for opioids in the treatment of arthritis," *Drugs* 62 (2002): 255–263.

Schiff, P.L. "Opium and its alkaloids," *American Journal of Pharmaceutical Education* 66 (2002): 186–194.

Wilkinson, G.R. "Drug metabolism and variability among patients in drug response," *New England Journal of Medicine* 352 (2005): 2211–2221.

Web sites

These sites, which were consulted by the author while researching and writing this book, may be useful to those interested in learning more about codeine.

American Pain Foundation
http://www.painfoundation.org

Narconon. FAQ About Codeine
http://www.drugrehabamerica.net/FAQ-codeine.htm

National Institute on Drug Abuse/NIDA for Teens
http://www.teens.drugabuse.gov/

National Institutes of Health Office of Science Education
http://science.education.nih.gov

Public Broadcasting Service (PBS)
http://www.pbs.org/wgbh/pages/frontline/shows/heroin/etc/history.html

Substance Abuse and Mental Health Administration
http://www.oas.samhsa.gov/nsduh.htm

Bibliography

Yale New Haven Health
http://yalenewhavenhealth.org

U.S. Department of Health and Human Services. Substance Abuse and Mental Health Administration, 2004 National Survey on Drug Use & Health. Substance Abuse and Mental Health Statistics
http://www.oas.samhsa.gov/nsduh.htm

U.S. Drug Enforcement Agency
http://www.dea.gov

U.S. Food and Drug Administration
http://www.fda.gov/cder/genomics

U.S. Food and Drug Administration
http://www.fda.gov/oc/history/default.htm

U.S. National Library of Medicine and the National Institutes of Health
http://www.nlm.nih.gov

U.S. National Library of Medicine and the National Institutes of Health, MedlinePlus
http://www.nlm.nih.gov/medlineplus/druginformation.html

Index

absorption, 26, 34, 36

abuse, 13, 64–68, 71–72, 74

acetaminophen, 23, 33, 70

activated charcoal, 61

acupuncture, 76, 78, 80, 81, 83

addiction, 13, 23, 32, 54, 65, 66. *See also* dependence

affinity, 29

agitation. *See* dysphoria

alcohol, 57, 63

alkaloid compound, 10–11, 13, 83

allergies, 18, 33

alternative medicine, 76–84

amino acids, 81

amphetamines, 57, 63

amygdale, 22

analgesia
  alternative therapies, 81, 83
  benefit of codeine, 48
  brain pathways involved in, 64
  codeine formulations and, 33–34
  controlling sensation of pain, 29
  drug action and, 42–47
  pain relief, 10, 13, 21–23
  primary use of codeine, 70

analgesic ladder, 23, 24

anesthetics, 57

animal testing, 49

antagonist, 61

antidepressants, 57

antidiarrheal. *See* diarrhea, controlling

antihistamine, 33, 57

antipsychotic drug, 11, 63

antipyretic, 33

antitussive, 20, 47, 83–84

See also cough suppression

aromatherapy, 76

arthritis, 22, 23, 42

Asians and drug metabolism, 39

aspirin, 21, 23, 33, 55, 70

asthma, 18

Ayurvedic medicine, 77, 78

barbiturate, 33, 57, 63

base, 38

base pairs, 38

benzodiazepine antianxiety drugs, 64

beta blockers, 57

binding sites, 45

Blacks and drug metabolism, 39

black tea and codeine absorption, 36

black walnut and codeine absorption, 36

blood plasma, 41

blood pressure, low. *See* hypotension

bone injury, 22

bovine colostrum, 84

bowel movement, 25

brain
  cough reflex and, 18
  diagram of, 16
  pain pathways, 22, 64
  structures of, 17
  transmission of pain, 45

Brewer's yeast, 84

bronchi/bronchial tubes, 15, 18

bronchodilators, 18

Brontex®, 21, 33

butalbital, 33

Butterbur, 83

butyrophenone, 63

caffeine, 33, 63

CAM on PubMed, 82

cancer pain, 22, 42

capsules, 21, 30–34

carcinogenic effect, 52

carob, 84

case study, codeine poisoning, 60

Caucasians and drug metabolism, 39

Center for Food Safety and Applied Nutrition, 83

central nervous system (CNS), 18, 22, 25, 62

cerebrum, 22

chemical compound, 10

Cheracol® with Codeine Syrup, 21, 72

childbirth pain, 22

Chinese medicine, 76, 78–81, 83

chiropractic, 76, 78, 81

chlophedianol, 20

chloral hydrate, 57, 63

chlorpromazine, 63

chronic pain, 22–23

chronic toxicity, 52

clearance of codeine, 40–41

clinical trials, 49, 74, 77, 80

CNS. *See* central nervous system

cocaine, 71, 74

cocoa leaves, 74

codeine
  complementary and alternative medicine, 76–84
  controlled substance, 69–75
  medicinal and cultural history, 10–14
  medicinal chemistry and pharmacology, 26–47
  physical properties of, 29

95

Index

Index

About the Author

Brigid M. Kane received her undergraduate degree in Biology from Virginia Polytechnic Institute & State University in Blacksburg, VA and her Masters degree from Temple University in Philadelphia, PA, where her focus was on cellular and developmental biology. After brief stints as a high school math and science teacher and then a biomedical research assistant, Brigid established herself as a science writer, working primarily in the fields of infectious diseases, HIV/AIDS, public health, oncology/hematology, and pharmaceutical science. She has authored articles for *Science* and the *Annals of Internal Medicine* and has prepared numerous clinical research manuscripts for peer-reviewed medical and scientific journals as well as continuing education manuscripts and projects for physicians and other healthcare professionals. Brigid lives in the Adirondack Mountains in Fulton County, New York.

About the Editor

David J. Triggle is a University Professor and a Distinguished Professor in the School of Pharmacy and Pharmaceutical Sciences at the State University of New York at Buffalo. He studied in the United Kingdom and earned his B.Sc. degree in Chemistry from the University of Southampton and a Ph.D. degree in Chemistry at the University of Hull. Following post-doctoral work at the University of Ottawa in Canada and the University of London in the United Kingdom, he assumed a position at the School of Pharmacy at Buffalo. He served as Chairman of the Department of Biochemical Pharmacology from 1971 to 1985 and as Dean of the School of Pharmacy from 1985 to 1995. From 1995 to 2001 he served as the Dean of the Graduate School, and as the University Provost from 2000 to 2001. He is the author of several books dealing with the chemical pharmacology of the autonomic nervous system and drug-receptor interactions, some 400 scientific publications, and has delivered over 1,000 lectures worldwide on his research.